Editor
Mara Ellen Guckian

Managing Editor
Ina Massler Levin, M.A.

Editor-in-Chief
Sharon Coan, M.S. Ed.

Illustrator
Sue Fullam

Cover Artist
Barb Lorseyedi

Art Coordinator
Denice Adorno

Imaging
Ralph Olmedo, Jr.
Alfred Lau

Product Manager
Phil Garcia

Publishers
Rachelle Cracchiolo, M.S. Ed.
Mary Dupuy Smith, M.S. Ed.

Teaching
Art and Music
through Nursery Rhymes

Authors

Jennifer Kern, M.A. and Amy DeCastro, M.A.

Teacher Created Materials, Inc.
6421 Industry Way
Westminster, CA 92683
www.teachercreated.com
ISBN-0-7439-3011-X
©2001 Teacher Created Materials, Inc.
Made in U.S.A.

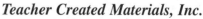

Table of Contents

Introduction

Many of the most important academic skills that young students learn are based upon skills learned through art standards. The goal of this book is to assist primary teachers in developing in their students the skills of perceiving, thinking, and image making (forming) through thematic, skill-based nursery rhyme lessons.

Students will also experience music through the activities in this book. They will become acquainted with the qualities of music that make sound expressive. Their understanding of these qualities—such as long/short, loud/soft, high/low, fast/slow—is an important part of music reading readiness. When combined, this literature-based, hands-on approach to learning is not only fun but meets many standards and criteria that students need to know in order to develop in other curricular areas. Learning the nursery rhymes themselves helps students develop phonemic awareness, increases vocabulary and verbal skills, and develops strong auditory discrimination. There are levels of information and understanding regarding art and music that can be enhanced at this early stage of learning as well.

The developmentally appropriate nursery rhyme activities in this book are created to easily integrate art and music standards into the curriculum. Such integration enriches learning and makes it meaningful and holistic. With a link to literature, these authentic lessons prepare students for art and music understanding in an enjoyable and natural way.

Teaching Art and Music through Nursery Rhymes was organized with easy-to-follow, step-by-step plans. Each art and music lesson lists objectives taught, and each music lesson includes an integration of language arts—including letter recognition and practice, along with hand signs for each letter. An alphabet song page is also included for an easy-to-find reference to letter jingles, which will also allow for easy access when using them in other curricular activities. The art lessons focus on real art objectives which result in quality learning experiences in art. The step-by-step procedures are easy to follow to ensure success. Teachers can also feel confident knowing that students are achieving the skills expected.

The information in this book will provide a wealth of hands-on experiences for young learners. Modify the lessons to fit the needs of your students or your individualized curriculum. Most of all, have fun with art and music!

Alphabet Song

by Jennifer Kern and Amy DeCastro

arranged by Craig Scribner

Alphabet Song (cont.)

L, lamb, Ma–ry's lamb, fol–lowed her to school, she's in a jam!

M, Muf–fet, Lit–tle Miss! would not give that spi–der a kiss!

N, nut–meg, nut–meg and pear would my lit–tle nut tree bear?

O, old, old wo–man in a shoe, had so man–y kids, what's she gon–na do?

P, peep at Lit–tle Bo–Peep.(If) She's not care–ful she'll lose her sheep!

Q, quick, Jack be quick, Jack jump o–ver the can–dle–stick!

R, run, run up the hill but don't fall down with Jack and Jill!

S, Si–mon, Sim–ple Si–mon, we all know he met a pie–man!

T, tea, let's all have tea! Pol–ly put the ket–tle on for you and me!

U, un–der, un–der the hay, Lit–tle Boy Blue was sleep–ing a–way.

V, ve–ry crook–ed mouse and a crook–ed man in a crook–ed house.

Alphabet Song *(cont.)*

W,   wall,   off   the   wall.   Hump – ty   Dump – ty   had   a   great   fall!

X,   ex – tra,   have you ex – tra   wool?   Yes   sir!   Yes   sir!   Three   bags   full.

Y,   Yan – kee   dood – le dee   dee!   Went   to   town   on   his   lit – tle   po –   ny.

Z,   ze – ro   roast beef   had he,   for   the   lit – tle   pig who went   wee   wee   wee!

Teaching Tips

Children love music of all kinds. Here are a few ideas to begin introducing basic concepts to young musicians.

♪ High and Low Notes

Point out to the children that they can see high and low things. In the classroom, they can see the light fixture on the ceiling, and they can see a pencil on the floor. Explain that we can also have high and low movement. Pretend to tie your shoe. This would illustrate low. Then point out that music can be high and low.

♪ Fast and Slow

Have the children form a circle holding hands. Begin by walking slowly to the right. Stop. Explain that just like walking, music can move slowly. Next, begin walking slowly and then walk slightly faster. Stop. Explain that music can go fast. Sing the jingle for the rhyme slowly. Have the children walk around the circle to the beat of the jingle. Say it again faster. See if the students can hear the faster beat, responding by walking faster. Ask, Did you hear the music go faster? Did you walk faster?

♪ Steady Beat

Make the symbol I I I I on the board, symbolizing four steady beats. Clap the beat for the students, showing them the symbols on the board. Have them repeat the steady beat back to you. Ask if they could show a steady beat in any other ways: Stomping, jumping, rhythm sticks, triangle, etc. Ask, What other things have a steady beat? (*clock ticking*)

♪ Loud and Soft

Brainstorm things that are loud and things that are soft. Make lists. Explain that music can be loud and soft also. Introduce the jingle. Explain that it is time to tiptoe to the beat of the jingle to illustrate "soft." Do it again, but this time illustrate "loud" by stomping the rhythm of the jingle. Do it a third time, this time nodding your head to the rhythm of the jingle. Was this loud or soft? Clap to the rhythm. Was this loud or soft?

Nursery Rhyme Scope and Sequence

Art Standards

Nursery Rhyme	Understands and applies media, techniques, and processes related to the visual arts	Knows how to use the structures and functions of art	Knows a range of subject matter, symbols, and potential ideas in the visual arts	Understands the characteristics and merits of one's own artwork and the artwork of others
This Little Piggie	X	X	X	X
Yankee Doodle	X	X	X	X
Baa, Baa, Black Sheep	X	X	X	X
Humpty Dumpty	X	X	X	X
There Was a Crooked Man	X	X	X	X X
Little Boy Blue	X	X	X	X X
Polly Put the Kettle On	X	X	X	X X
Simple Simon	X X	X	X X	X X
Jack and Jill	X	X	X	X X
Jack Be Nimble	X	X	X	X X
Little Bo-Peep	X X	X	X X	X X
There Was an Old Woman	X	X	X	X X
Little Nut Tree	X	X	X	X
Little Miss Muffet	X	X	X	X
Mary Had a Little Lamb	X	X	X	X
Georgie Porgie	X	X	X	X
Diddle, Diddle, Dumpling	X	X	X	X
Little Jack Horner	X	X	X	X
Pease Porridge Hot	X	X	X	X
Mary, Mary, Quite Contrary	X	X	X	X
Three Little Kittens	X	X	X	X
Peter, Peter, Pumpkin Eater	X	X	X	X X
Hey Diddle, Diddle	X	X	X	X X
Hickory, Dickory, Dock	X	X	X	X X
Three Men in a Tub	X X	X	X X	X X
Ring-Around-the-Rosies	X X	X	X X	X X

Nursery Rhyme Scope and Sequence

Music Standards

Nursery Rhyme	Sings alone and with others, a varied repertoire of music	Performs on instruments, alone and with others, a varied repertoire of music	Improvises melodies, variations, and accompaniments	Composes and arranges music within specified guidelines	Reads and notates music	Knows and applies appropriate criteria to music and music performances	Understands the relationship between music and history and culture
This Little Piggie	X		X			X	X
Yankee Doodle	X	X	X	X	X	X	X
Baa, Baa, Black Sheep	X	X	X	X	X	X	X
Humpty Dumpty	X	X	X	X	X	X	X
There Was a Crooked Man	X		X			X	X
Little Boy Blue	X				X	X	X
Polly Put the Kettle On	X		X			X	X
Simple Simon	X	X	X	X	X	X	X
Jack and Jill	X				X	X	X
Jack Be Nimble	X		X	X		X	X
Little Bo-Peep	X		X	X		X	X
There Was an Old Woman	X	X	X	X	X	X	X
Little Nut Tree	X		X			X	X
Little Miss Muffet	X		X			X	X
Mary Had a Little Lamb	X		X		X	X	X
Georgie Porgie	X				X		
Diddle, Diddle, Dumpling	X		X		X	X	
Little Jack Horner	X	X	X	X	X	X	X
Pease Porridge Hot	X		X			X	X
Mary, Mary, Quite Contrary	X	X	X	X	X	X	X
Three Little Kittens	X		X			X	X
Peter, Peter, Pumpkin Eater	X		X		X	X	X
Hey Diddle, Diddle	X	X	X	X	X	X	X
Hickory, Dickory, Dock	X		X		X	X	X
Three Men in a Tub	X		X		X	X	X
Ring-Around-the-Rosies	X		X		X	X	X

Ring-Around-the-Rosies

Ring-around-the-rosies

A pocket full of posies

Ashes, ashes,

We all fall down!

Ring-Around-the-Rosies (cont.)

Art Lesson

Skills

- creates texture
- uses lines to create a recognizable object

Materials

- salt and empty shakers
- rose pattern (page 11), one per student
- pink and green sidewalk chalk
- 2 medium bowls
- glue
- pencils, one per student
- 6" x 18" (15 cm x 46 cm) construction paper in yellow, light blue, or white, one per student
- baking pan

Before the Lesson

1. Copy and enlarge the nursery rhyme "Ring-Around-the-Rosies" (page 9) onto butcher paper or chart paper. Display in the classroom.
2. Copy the rose pattern for each student.

Procedure

1. Read the nursery rhyme "Ring-Around-the-Rosies" to the students. Read the rhyme again, inviting the students to join in, tracking the words as they are read. Explain that a "rosie" can be created using a technique similar to sand art.
2. Pour ¹/₂ cup (100 g) of salt into one bowl. Stir the salt with a stick of pink chalk. The salt will begin to turn pink after a few minutes of stirring. Students may take turns stirring the salt. The more it is stirred, the more colorful the salt will be. Put the pink salt into a shaker.
3. Pour ¹/₂ cup (100 g) of salt into another bowl. Stir the salt with a stick of green chalk. The salt will begin to turn green. Put the green salt into another shaker.
4. Cut out and assemble the rose on the construction paper. Outline and fill the flower with glue.
5. Lay the paper in a tray and shake the pink salt over the top of the flower on the glue.
6. Shake the excess salt off of the picture. Empty the excess salt in the tray back into the bowl.
7. Outline and fill in the stem and leaves with glue. Lay the paper in the tray and shake the green salt over the glue.
8. Shake the excess salt off of the picture. Empty the excess salt in the tray back into the bowl.
9. Allow the art work to dry overnight. Display the finished flowers.

Ring-Around-the-Rosies (cont.)

Art Lesson (cont.)

Ring-Around-the-Rosies (cont.)

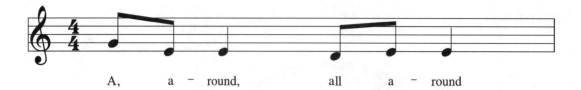

A,   a - round,   all   a - round

Ring a-round-the - ro - sies and we   all   fall   down!

Music Lesson

Skills

- differentiates between fast and slow music
- recognizes the sound /a/
- knows the hand sign for the letter "a"

Materials

- large open area
- music
- butcher paper or chart paper

Before the Lesson

1. Copy and enlarge the jingle for the letter "a" onto butcher paper or chart paper.

2. Copy and enlarge the nursery rhyme "Ring-Around-the-Rosies" from page 9 onto butcher paper or chart paper.

Procedure

1. Read the nursery rhyme "Ring-Around-the-Rosies" to the class. Read the rhyme a second time, inviting the students to join in as you track the words on the chart.

2. Divide the class into groups of four or five. Practice the traditional "Ring-Around-the-Rosies" dance by holding hands in small groups, circling around, and falling down on knees when the rhyme says "all fall down." Practice the dance while reciting the rhyme a few times.

3. Meet at the gathering area. Using the chart of the jingle for the letter "a," read the jingle to the class. Explain to students that this jingle is similar to the nursery rhyme "Ring-Around-the-Rosies," but that this one will help them to remember one sound that the letter "a" makes as in *around.* Say the jingle together, tracking the words on the chart as they are read.

Ring-Around-the-Rosies *(cont.)*

Music Lesson *(cont.)*

Procedure *(cont.)*

4. Show the students the hand sign for the letter "a." (See example.) Explain that this is the sign that is used to represent the letter "a" for those who cannot hear or speak. This will also help them to remember "a" as the sign is made during the jingle. Say the jingle again, using the hand sign for "a" when "a" is read on the chart.

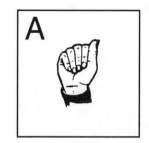

5. Go back to groups of four or five and repeat the jingle again while doing the traditional "Ring-Around-the-Rosies" dance.

6. Introduce slow music by explaining that the next time they do the "Ring-Around-the-Rosies" dance and sing the letter "a" jingle, they are going to say it very slow, and they will also make their circle move very slowly. Try the jingle slowly.

7. Introduce fast music by explaining that the next time they do the "Ring-Around-the-Rosies" dance and sing the letter "a" jingle, they are going to say it very fast, and their circle will move faster than before. Try the jingle quickly.

8. Repeat as many times as desired.

Three Men in a Tub

Rub a dub, dub

Three men in a tub

And who do you think they be?

The butcher, the baker,

The candlestick maker

Turn 'em out, knaves all three!

Three Men in a Tub (cont.)

Art Lesson

Skills

- explores the pliability and dimensionality of clay
- explores the possibilities given by clay
- completes an expressive form appropriate to the student's maturation level
- creates soap clay

Materials

- dry soap powder or detergent
- water
- bowls, one per student
- butcher paper or chart paper

Before the Lesson

1. Copy and enlarge the nursery rhyme "Three Men in a Tub" (page 14) onto butcher paper or chart paper and display in the classroom.

2. Gather enough ingredients for each student to have a small handful of dough. Use ¹/₂ cup (120 mL) of water for every 2 cups (450 g) of soap. If necessary, add more soap to create a ball with a dough-like consistency.

Procedure

1. Read the nursery rhyme "Three Men in a Tub" to the class, using an enlarged version of page 14. Read the nursery rhyme again, inviting the students to join in while tracking the words as they are read.

2. Discuss the nursery rhyme. Ask, What do you think "Rub a dub, dub" means? Have you heard that phrase before? Direct students to the understanding that the men may be taking a bath and getting clean. Who was in the tub? (*the butcher, the baker, and the candlestick maker*) What do you think "Turn 'em out, knaves all three" means?

3. Direct students to the understanding that the men in the tub may be pretending to be pirates on a ship. Do you think men would really be playing and pretending in a tub, or do you think that this may be a nursery rhyme about students pretending to be men in a tub? Do you ever play in the tub?

Three Men in a Tub (cont.)

Art Lesson (cont.)

Procedure (cont.)

4. Explain to the students that today they will "rub a dub, dub" with soap and water while making clay. Model for the students as you mix the soap and water together, creating a dough-like texture. Show the students how they can practice making different shapes with the mixture.

5. Send students to their work areas. Give each student a bowl with 1 cup (225 g) of dry soap or detergent in it. Pour a small amount of water (approximately $^1/_4$ cup [60 mL]) in each student's bowl. Encourage the students to mix the dough with their fingers. Observe students as they do this, adding more soap or water to their mixtures to create a dough-like consistency.

6. Allow students to experiment with their dough, creating new shapes and forms.

7. When finished, allow the forms to dry. These will make great soap balls to use at home! Rinse hands. They should smell very clean! Rub a dub, dub!

Three Men in a Tub (cont.)

Music Lesson

Skills

- differentiates between loud and soft music
- knows the hand sign for the letter "b"
- recognizes the sound /b/

Materials

- butcher paper or chart paper

Before the Lesson

1. Copy and enlarge the jingle for the letter "b" onto butcher paper or chart paper.
2. Copy and enlarge the nursery rhyme "Three Men in a Tub" from page 14 onto butcher paper or chart paper.

Procedure

1. Read the nursery rhyme "Three Men in a Tub" to the class. Read the rhyme a second time, inviting the students to join in as you track the words on the chart.

2. Divide the class into groups of three. Let them role-play the nursery rhyme by pretending to sit in a tub together, rowing with their pretend oars as they say the nursery rhyme out loud.

3. Meet at the gathering area. Using the chart of the jingle for the letter "b," read the jingle to the class. Explain to students that this jingle is similar to the nursery rhyme "Three Men in a Tub," but that this one will help them to remember the sound that the letter "b" makes as in *butcher* and *baker*. Say the jingle together, tracking the words on the chart as they are read.

4. Show the students the sign for the letter "b." See example. Explain that this is the sign used to represent the letter "b" for those who cannot hear or talk. This will also help them to remember "b" as they make this sign during the jingle. Repeat the jingle, using the hand sign for "b" when "b" is read on the chart.

5. Go back to groups of three and repeat the jingle again while pretending to row a tub.

6. Introduce loud music by explaining that the next time they do the jingle in their pretend tubs, they will say it very loudly. Try the jingle, singing it loudly.

7. Introduce soft music by explaining that the next time they do the jingle in their pretend tubs, they will sing it very softly. Try the jingle, singing it softly. Repeat as many times as desired.

Hickory, Dickory, Dock

Hickory, dickory, dock,

The mouse ran up the clock.

The clock struck one,

The mouse ran down,

Hickory, dickory, dock.

Hickory, Dickory, Dock *(cont.)*

Art Lesson

Skills

- creates the illusion of texture
- uses line to create recognizable figures
- creates prints by using a rubbing process

Materials

- black marker, one per student
- pencils, one per student
- thin white copy paper, one per student
- variety of textured surfaces (braided place mats, brick, lace tablecloths, corrugated cardboard, etc.)
- "How to Draw a Mouse" strip
- butcher paper or chart paper

Before the Lesson

1. Copy and enlarge the nursery rhyme "Hickory, Dickory, Dock" from page 18 onto butcher paper or chart paper. Display it in the classroom.
2. Copy and enlarge the "How to Draw a Mouse" strip on butcher paper.

Procedure

1. Read the nursery rhyme "Hickory, Dickory, Dock," using the enlarged version. Reread the rhyme, inviting the students to join you in tracking the words as you say them.
2. Explain that we are going to draw the little mouse that ran up the clock and then create texture on his fur coat.
3. Show the students the "How to Draw a Mouse" chart. Explain that they do not have to use the chart, but it is a guide if they should need it. It shows ways to turn simple shapes into a recognizable figure. Explain that the figure will need to be adjusted to the size of their paper. Model for the students as you draw the mouse.
4. Trace the pencil markings with black marker so that they will show up after the color is added.
5. Choose a textured surface to place underneath the paper. Color the mouse. The textured surface underneath will create a surface that looks textured, but still feels smooth.

How to Draw a Mouse

Hickory, Dickory, Dock *(cont.)*

C,   clock,   hick‑'ry dick‑ory dock,   the

mouse   runs   up   as it goes   tick   tock!

Music Lesson

Skills

- keeps a steady beat
- knows the hand sign for the letter "c"
- recognizes the sound /c/ (hard c sound)

Before the Lesson

1. Copy and enlarge the jingle for the letter "c" onto butcher paper or chart paper.

2. Copy and enlarge the nursery rhyme "Hickory, Dickory, Dock" (page 18) onto butcher paper or chart paper.

Materials

- wind-up egg timer
- metronome
- butcher paper or chart paper

Procedure

1. Read the nursery rhyme "Hickory, Dickory, Dock" to the class. Read the rhyme a second time, inviting the students to join in as you track the words on the chart.

2. Show the students the metronome. Turn it on as they listen to the steady beats that it makes. See if they can keep the same beat as the metronome as they clap. Practice keeping the same steady beat as they make clicking sounds with their mouths. Ask them for suggestions of different things they could do to keep a steady beat. Explain that just like the clock in "Hickory, Dickory, Dock," this metronome keeps a steady beat.

Hickory, Dickory, Dock *(cont.)*

Music Lesson *(cont.)*

Procedure *(cont.)*

3. Turn on the timer and put it up to your ear. Explain to the students that a timer will also keep a steady beat. It doesn't start going faster or slower, but stays the same. Pass the timer around so that all students can have a chance to listen to the timer. Discuss other times that they may have heard a watch ticking or a clock ticking.

4. Begin clapping at a slow and steady beat. Ask the students to join you in this slow and steady beat. While clapping the beat, begin reciting the nursery rhyme "Hickory, Dickory, Dock." Encourage students to join in with you.

5. Show students the chart containing the jingle for the letter "c." Explain to the students that this jingle is similar to the nursery rhyme "Hickory, Dickory, Dock," but that this one will help them to remember the sound that the letter "c" makes as in *clock*. Read the jingle to the class. Sing the jingle together, tracking the words as they are read.

6. Show the students the hand sign for the letter "c." (See example.) Explain that this is the sign used to represent the letter "c" for people who cannot hear or speak. This will also help them to remember "c" as they make this sign during the jingle. Sing the jingle again, using the hand sign for "c" when "c" is read on the chart.

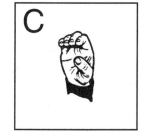

7. Sing the jingle again, keeping a steady clapping beat (four slow claps per verse). Invite students to take turns doing the jingle for each other.

Hey Diddle, Diddle

Hey Diddle, Diddle,

The cat and the fiddle,

The cow jumped over the moon.

The little dog laughed

To see such a sport,

And the dish ran away

with the spoon.

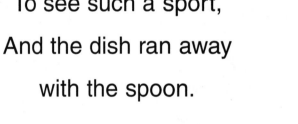

Hey Diddle, Diddle (cont.)

Art Lesson 1

Skills

- recognizes that there are differences in media techniques and processes
- uses different media techniques and processes to create art
- explores how different artworks express different ideas
- uses visual structures of art to communicate ideas
- recognizes that meaning can be communicated through use of subject matter, symbols, and ideas

Materials

- cow and barn patterns (page 25)
- craft sticks, one per student
- aluminum pie pans, one per group
- vinegar and water
- blue and green oil-based paint
- turpentine (teacher use only)
- paintbrushes
- stick for stirring
- scissors
- glue
- white fabric paint
- white paper plates, one per student
- 3" (8 cm) square orange construction paper pieces, one per student

Before the Lesson

1. In a bowl, mix a small amount of blue paint with enough turpentine so that the paint shakes from the brush easily. Do the same with the green paint.
2. Fill a pie pan with water. Add a few drops of vinegar to it.
3. Copy or enlarge the nursery rhyme "Hey Diddle, Diddle" (page 22) onto butcher paper or chart paper. Display it in the classroom.
4. Copy the cow and barn patterns for each student.

Procedure

1. Read the nursery rhyme "Hey Diddle, Diddle," using the enlarged version of the rhyme. Read the rhyme a second time, tracking the words and allowing the students to join in if they already know the words.

Hey Diddle, Diddle *(cont.)*

Art Lesson 1 *(cont.)*

Procedure *(cont.)*

2. Discuss with the students what nighttime looks like.

   - What colors do you see at night?
   - What types of things do you see in the sky?
   - Is nighttime the same every night?
   - What types of things change when you look in the sky?

   Ask, What part of the rhyme "Hey Diddle, Diddle" takes part at nighttime? (*The cow jumped over the moon.*) How do you know? (*Because the moon comes out at nighttime.*) Explain that we are going to experiment with a procedure that will produce nighttime-looking sky.

3. Using the tray of water and vinegar, model for the students how they will flick small droplets of blue and green paint in the water with a paintbrush. Stir the mixture gently with a paintbrush so that the paint begins to swirl around.

4. Lay a paper plate in the vinegar, water, and paint mixture. Wait a couple of seconds and lift out the plate. Lay the plate out to dry. This will create the nighttime background that you will need for the farm scene.

5. While the plate is drying, cut out and color the cow and barn patterns from page 25. Glue the cow pattern to a craft stick.

6. Glue the barn to the lower right hand corner of the paper plate.

7. Cut a circle (the moon) from the orange construction paper. Glue this to the upper corner of the plate.

8. Using white fabric paint, create a picket fence with straight lines across the bottom of the plate. Cross the straight lines with two horizontal lines. This will create a farm scene. Allow the fabric paint to dry for two hours.

9. When the plate is dry and ready to use, glue the smaller version of the nursery rhyme from page 22 to the back side of the plate. Gluing three sides of the nursery rhyme down and leaving the top open will create a pocket in which to keep the cow puppet when it is not in use.

10. Recite the nursery rhyme, using the cow puppet that you made to jump over the moon at the appropriate time. This will provide a hands-on review of the nursery rhyme and a wonderful experience with paint.

Hey Diddle, Diddle (cont.)

Art Lesson 1 *(cont.)*

Cow and Barn Patterns

Hey Diddle, Diddle *(cont.)*

Art Lesson 2

Skills

- creates and uses a musical instrument
- follows directions

Materials

- rubber bands, three per student
- paint stir sticks or rulers, one per student
- sticks for bows, one per student
- paintbrushes
- sample of fiddle music
- tissue boxes (rectangular), one per student
- hot glue gun/hot glue
- tempera paint
- butcher paper or chart paper
- pictures of fiddles

Teacher Note: Teachers and other adults should always be at hand to apply hot glue. Students should not use the hot glue guns themselves.

Before the Lesson

1. Copy and enlarge the rhyme "Hey Diddle, Diddle" from page 22 onto chart paper for the whole class to view during the lesson.

2. Paint one tissue box for a class example.

3. Enlarge, color, and cut out the fiddle on this page.

Procedure

1. Read the nursery rhyme "Hey Diddle, Diddle" to the class, using the larger version prepared on chart paper. Read the rhyme again and invite the students to read it with you.

2. Ask, Does anyone know what a fiddle is? Take answers. Discuss the rhyme, pointing out that the fiddle is a musical instrument. Show examples of fiddles. Explain that a fiddle is a string instrument that looks a little bit like a guitar, but is actually played with a bow rather than fingers. If available, play a sample of fiddle music.

Hey Diddle, Diddle (cont.)

Art Lesson 2 (cont.)

Procedure (cont.)

3. Explain that they are going to make fiddles like the one in the nursery rhyme "Hey Diddle, Diddle," using a tissue box, rubber bands, and a ruler. (Hold up objects to be used in the lesson.) Explain to the students that the tissue box used as the sample has already been painted with tempera paint and that they will have the opportunity to paint their own boxes later.

4. Model for the students how to wrap the rubber bands once. (See sample.)

5. Using hot glue, attach the ruler to the back of the box across the rubber bands. This will keep the rubber bands in place.

6. Pull each rubber band to illustrate to the students how rubber bands make sounds. Hold the wooden stick to the rubber bands, pulling it across them to illustrate how a fiddler would make sounds with his bow.

7. Pass out paint supplies and rubber bands. Explain to the students that an adult will need to attach the ruler onto their fiddles with hot glue after they dry. Encourage students to place rubber bands around their tissue boxes before painting to avoid mess.

8. Allow box fiddles to dry for one to two hours.

9. Take turns playing the fiddles. If possible, accompany fiddle music listened to earlier.

Hey Diddle, Diddle (cont.)

D, did – dle, hey did – dle, did – dle

what's a cow to do with a cat and a fid – dle?

Music Lesson

Skills

- uses self-made musical instruments
- knows the hand sign for the letter "d"
- recognizes the sound /d/

Materials

- student-made fiddles from Art Lesson 2 (pages 26 and 27)
- copy of letter "d" jingle
- enlarged copy of nursery rhyme (page 22)
- wooden sticks to use as bows

Before the Lesson

Copy and enlarge the jingle for the letter "d" onto butcher paper or chart paper.

Procedure

1. Read the nursery rhyme "Hey Diddle, Diddle," using the enlarged version from Art Lesson 1. Reread the nursery rhyme, tracking the words on the chart and allowing students who feel comfortable reciting the rhyme to join in.

2. Ask, What is a fiddle? How does a fiddle relate to this rhyme?

3. Write the letter "d" on chart paper. Ask, Can anyone tell me what this letter is? Take answers.

4. Introduce the letter "d" jingle, using the enlarged version. Explain to the students that this one will help them to remember the sound that the letter "d" makes as in *dog*. Read the jingle to the class. Sing the jingle together, tracking the words.

5. Read the rhyme a second time, clapping the beat with your hands. Invite students to join you as you repeat the rhyme a third time, clapping the beat with their hands.

6. Introduce the hand sign for the letter "d." Explain that this is the sign used to communicate the letter "d" for those who cannot hear or speak.

7. Hand each student their fiddle and bow. Model for the students how to play the fiddle on the beat that they have learned for the letter "d" jingle. Pull the bow up for one beat and down for another. Invite students to experiment with their fiddles.

8. Practice reciting and playing fiddles to the rhythm of the letter "d" jingle.

Peter, Peter, Pumpkin Eater

Peter, Peter, pumpkin eater

Had a wife and couldn't

Keep her.

He put her in a pumpkin shell,

And there he kept her very well.

Peter, Peter, Pumpkin Eater *(cont.)*

Art Lesson 1

Skills
- creates texture by tearing paper and applying it to paper
- compares surface textures and can identify *rough, smooth, soft,* and *bumpy*
- understands that texture is the quality of a surface

Materials
- 9" x 12" (23 cm x 30 cm) orange construction paper, one per student
- 6" (15 cm) square green tissue paper, one per student
- 12" (30 cm) square of yellow, black, or white construction paper for background, one per student
- 10" (25 cm) square orange tissue paper, one per student
- copy of "Peter, Peter, Pumpkin Eater" nursery rhyme
- copy of "How to Draw a Pumpkin" (page 32)
- pencils, one per student
- large pumpkin
- chart paper or butcher paper
- glue

Before the Lesson
1. Copy or enlarge the nursery rhyme "Peter, Peter, Pumpkin Eater" (page 29) onto chart paper or butcher paper so that the entire class will be able to view the rhyme as it is read.
2. Copy and enlarge "How to Draw a Pumpkin" onto chart paper so that the entire class will be able to see it.

Procedure
1. Read the nursery rhyme "Peter, Peter, Pumpkin Eater" to the class. Read the rhyme again. Track the words and invite the students who know the rhyme to join in reading it with you.
2. Discuss the rhyme. Ask questions about color, such as: What color are pumpkins? What color are the vines and stems that are attached to them?
3. Explain that they will re-create Peter's pumpkin using torn pieces of paper. This process is known to artists as *collage.* Collage means that pieces of things are pasted on a flat surface. Since pumpkins have orange and green on them, each child will get a piece of green paper and a piece of orange paper. The background paper for this project is variable, and white, black, or yellow are colors that would be complimentary to the finished piece. Explain that when things are done in collage, texture is created. They will be able to feel their pictures.

Peter, Peter, Pumpkin Eater *(cont.)*

Art Lesson 1 *(cont.)*

4. Discuss the shape of a pumpkin as a large pumpkin is passed from one student to another so that each may feel the texture, study the shape, and observe the colors present in a real pumpkin. Discuss other textures such as things that might have a rough, bumpy, smooth, or soft surface.

5. Show the students the chart, "How to Draw a Pumpkin." Remind them that pumpkins come in several shapes and sizes. The pumpkins that they will create do not have to be exactly the same as the pumpkin pictured or the same as the real pumpkin that was observed. The chart is to give them an idea of how to create the shapes that a pumpkin contains.

6. Model for the students the appropriate way to follow the "How to Draw a Pumpkin" chart by making a larger version on chart paper with a pencil. Have students cut out their pumpkin drawings.

7. Lay the cutout pumpkin on a flat surface. Begin the next step by filling in the stem area with glue.

8. Tear tiny pieces $\frac{1}{2}$" (1.3 cm) of the green tissue paper and place them in the stem area on the glue.

9. Fill in a portion of the pumpkin area with glue (approximately $\frac{1}{4}$ of it). Tear off tiny pieces of the orange piece of construction paper, placing them onto the glue in the pumpkin area. Repeat this process until the entire pumpkin area is covered with orange construction paper.

10. Display "Peter's Pumpkins" to show how many wonderful shapes and sizes pumpkins can be!

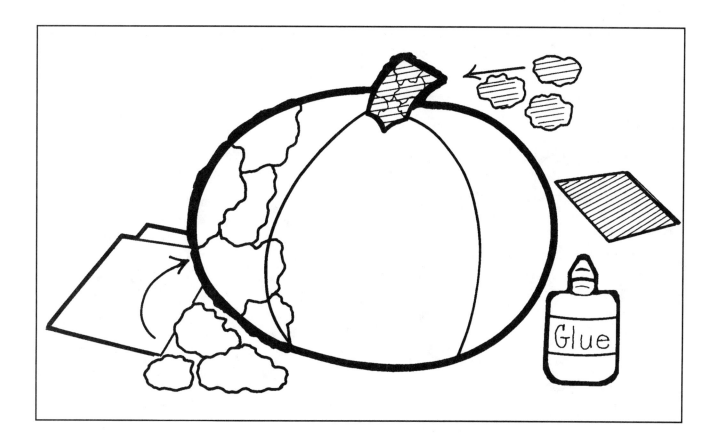

Peter, Peter, Pumpkin Eater *(cont.)*

How to Draw a Pumpkin

1. Draw a half-circle.

2. Draw another half-circle.

3. Draw a stem.

4. Add lines to shape the pumpkin.

Peter, Peter, Pumpkin Eater *(cont.)*

Art Lesson 2

Skills

- understands simple printmaking processes
- creates original prints
- demonstrates confidence in his or her creative ability
- understands the value of art and the printmaking medium
- understands that printmaking is the process of reproducing from a modified surface
- appreciates that printmaking is the oldest reproducible art form

Materials

- small pumpkins
- white tempera paint
- glue
- 12" x 18" (30 cm x 46 cm) orange construction paper, one per student
- knife (for adult use only)
- paper towels
- glitter
- paper plate, one per student
- butcher paper or chart paper
- forks, two per pumpkin

Before the Lesson

1. Copy and enlare the nursery rhyme "Peter, Peter, Pumpkin Eater" (page 29) onto butcher paper.

2. Put white tempera paint on the paper plate. Add half as much white glue and mix it together. Spread the paint/glue mixture on the plate.

Procedure

1. Read the rhyme "Peter, Peter, Pumpkin Eater." Reread the rhyme, tracking the words so students who feel comfortable reciting the rhyme with you may do so.

2. While students are watching, use the knife to cut the pumpkins in half horizontally, cleaning out the seeds inside to prepare the shells for printing. Explain that they will actually use a "pumpkin shell" just as Peter did to do the art lesson.

Peter, Peter, Pumpkin Eater *(cont.)*

Art Lesson 2 *(cont.)*

Procedure *(cont.)*

3. Discuss with the students that the process that they are going to learn about is a process called printmaking. *Printmaking* is the process of reproducing from a modified surface. Explain that a print can be made with almost anything. Printmaking is the oldest reproducible art form.

4. There are many different types of procedures for reproducing pictures such as copy machines. The type of printmaking that they will do today has been done for many years using many different objects. Ask, Have you ever made a fingerprint or a handprint on a window? Have you ever made a footprint in the sand? When you make prints, you are making copies of the original object in a new form.

5. Turn each pumpkin half over so that the outer shell is up. Poke a fork in the center of each one. Explain that this will be the handle that will be used. Model for the students how to dip the pumpkin shell into the white paint and then onto the orange paper. Discuss the print that was made. Make several prints on the paper.

6. Model for the students how to sprinkle glitter on the prints for a glittery contrast.

Peter, Peter, Pumpkin Eater *(cont.)*

Music Lesson

Skills

- identifies rhymes that go up and down
- recognizes the sound /e/
- knows the hand sign for the letter "e"

Before the Lesson

1. Copy and enlarge the jingle for the letter "e" onto butcher paper or chart paper.
2. Copy and enlarge the nursery rhyme "Peter, Peter Pumpkin Eater" from page 29 onto butcher paper or chart paper.

Procedure

1. Read the nursery rhyme "Peter, Peter Pumpkin Eater" to the class. Read the rhyme a second time, inviting the students to join in as you track the words on the chart.

2. Explain to the students that "Peter, Peter, Pumpkin Eater" is often shared as a song. Sing the song to the students.

Peter, Peter, Pumpkin Eater
Had a wife and couldn't keep her.
Put her in a pumpkin shell and
There he kept her ver-y well!

3. Point out how the notes go up and down in this song. Practice listening for notes as they go up and down by singing the song and standing up when the notes go up and squatting down when the notes go down. Did you find yourself standing up and squatting down quite a lot? This song includes many notes that go up and down.

Peter, Peter, Pumpkin Eater *(cont.)*

Music Lesson *(cont.)*

Procedure *(cont.)*

4. Introduce the jingle for the letter "e," using the enlarged chart. Read the jingle to the class. Explain to students that this jingle is similar to the nursery rhyme "Peter, Peter Pumpkin Eater," but that this one will help them to remember the sound that the letter "e" makes in the word *eat*. Say the jingle together, tracking the words on the chart as they are read.

5. Show the students the hand sign for the letter "e." (See example.) Explain that this is the sign that is used to represent the letter "e" for those who cannot hear or talk. This will also help them to remember "e" as they make this sign during the jingle. Say the jingle again, using the hand sign for "e" when "e" is read on the chart.

6. Ask, Did you hear the notes in this jingle go up and down as you said them? Try the standing/squatting exercise with this jingle.

7. Play a game for extra practice. Using a keyboard or bells, have students come up one at a time to play a note. If the note is high, the rest of the class may stand up. If the note is low, the class may squat down. If it is hard to tell whether the note is high or low, or it is in-between, sit in a chair.

Three Little Kittens

Three little kittens,
They lost their mittens,
And they began to cry.
Oh, mother dear, we sadly fear
Our mittens we have lost.
What, lost your mittens?
You naughty kittens!
Then you shall have no pie.
Mee-ow, mee-ow, mee-ow,
Then you shall have no pie.
The three little kittens,
They found their mittens,
And they began to cry.
Oh, mother dear, see here, see here,
Our mittens we have found!
Put on your mittens,
You silly kittens,
And you shall have some pie.
Purr-r, purr-r, purr-r
Oh, let us have some pie.

Three Little Kittens (cont.)

Art Lesson 1

Skills

- identifies basic shapes (circle, oval, triangle)
- is aware that a two-dimensional shape is formed when a line comes around and meets itself
- discovers that shapes can be put together to create a recognizable object

Materials

- large piece of white butcher paper for each student
- large pieces of colored butcher paper for students who choose to paint white cats
- copy of "How to Draw a Kitten," page 40
- yellow, orange, black, white, and brown tempera paint
- paintbrushes, one per student
- pencils, one per student
- paper cup (one per child or one per every two students sharing the same color)
- butcher paper or chart paper

Before the Lesson

1. Copy or enlarge the nursery rhyme "Three Little Kittens" (page 37) onto butcher paper or chart paper. Display it in the classroom.
2. Enlarge the "How to Draw a Kitten" onto butcher paper so that the students can see it and follow the directions from their workspaces.

Procedure

1. Read the nursery rhyme "Three Little Kittens," using the enlarged version of the rhyme. Read the rhyme a second time, tracking the words and allowing the students to join in if they already know the words.
2. Explain to the students that they will be making a version of a little kitten, except that this one will be BIG! Discuss with the students what colors real kittens could be. List those suggestions on chart paper.
3. Show the students the colors of tempera paint that are available to see if they match the suggestions that they gave.

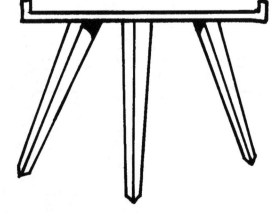

Three Little Kittens

Three little kittens,
They lost their mittens,
And they began to cry.
Oh, mother dear, we sadly fear
Our mittens we have lost.
What, lost your mittens?
You naughty kittens!
Then you shall have no pie.
Mee-ow, mee-ow, mee-ow,
Then you shall have no pie.

Three Little Kittens *(cont.)*

Art Lesson 1 *(cont.)*

Procedure *(cont.)*

4. Begin modeling the procedure by following the directions on the "How to Draw a Kitten" sheet with a pencil while the students watch. Make sure to draw it large enough to fill the entire space of the paper. This will show the students that they also need to enlarge their kittens quite a bit.

5. Choose a paint color and paint your kitten.

6. After the entire kitten is painted, go back in with black paint and place the eyes, nose, mouth, and whiskers on the kitten's face.

7. Hang or allow to dry at the workspace. The students will love their kittens! As an added feature, students could add glitter collars on their kittens after they dry.

8. Give students an opportunity to show their finished projects and talk about them.

Three Little Kittens *(cont.)*

How to Draw a Kitten

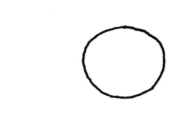

1. Draw a circle at the top for the face.

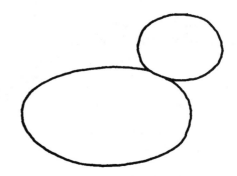

2. Draw a larger oval at the bottom.

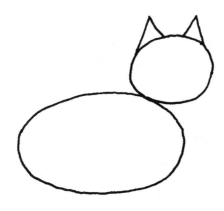

3. Draw two triangles for ears.

4. Draw eyes, nose, mouth, and whiskers.

5. Draw feet and a tail.

6. Paint the kitten.

Three Little Kittens *(cont.)*

Art Lesson 2

Skills

- demonstrates cutting skills
- designs paper into an expressive art object
- shows an awareness, through paper sculpture activities, of how artists make design decisions and see themselves as artists

Materials

- assortment of mittens to use as samples
- large-hole, plastic darning needles
- mitten pattern, page 42
- wallpaper sample books
- bag of cotton batting
- hole punch
- scissors
- tape
- yarn

Before the Lesson

1. Copy the mitten pattern from page 42 and cut it out. Trace the pattern onto cardstock or poster board. Make enough of these for students to share without a lot of waiting time. Cut them out for students to use for tracing.

2. Ask a nearby wallpaper store for discontinued wallpaper sample books to use in your classroom. You may want to tear the sheets out before the lesson for students to choose from more easily.

3. Copy or enlarge the nursery rhyme "Three Little Kittens" (page 37) onto butcher paper or chart paper. Display it in the classroom.

Procedure

1. Read the nursery rhyme "Three Little Kittens," using the enlarged version of the rhyme. Read the rhyme a second time, tracking the words and allowing the students to join in if they already know the words.

2. Lay several samples of mittens on the floor and ask, What do these have to do with the nursery rhyme "Three Little Kittens"? Take answers. What are some things that you notice about these mittens that are the same? What are some things that are different?

Three Little Kittens *(cont.)*

Art Lesson 2 *(cont.)*

Procedure *(cont.)*

3. Explain that they will be sewing their own mittens using wallpaper cutouts. Lay the wallpaper samples on the table or floor so students can see the different patterns available. Have students think about ways that they might use sewing techniques when they grow up. Discuss.

4. Model for the students the next three steps before letting them start on their own.

5. Choose two wallpaper samples. One sample will be used for the front of the mitten and the other will be used for the back of the mitten. Trace the mitten pattern on a wallpaper sample. Flip the pattern over to trace onto the other wallpaper sample. Make sure the design side of the sample is facedown when you do this. Cut out the mittens that you have traced.

6. Holding the mittens together with the design sides facing out, punch holes around the outside of the mittens, leaving the bottom edge free of holes.

7. Thread the needle with yarn and tape the yarn to the backside of the mitten, just below the thumb. Pass the needle through a hole, over and around the edge, and through the next hole in the mitten. Continue until the entire edge is finished with stitches. Then tape the free end of the yarn to the back of the mitten shape.

8. Stuff a handful of cotton batting inside the opening of the mitten.

9. Hang mittens to "dry" on a clothesline for display.

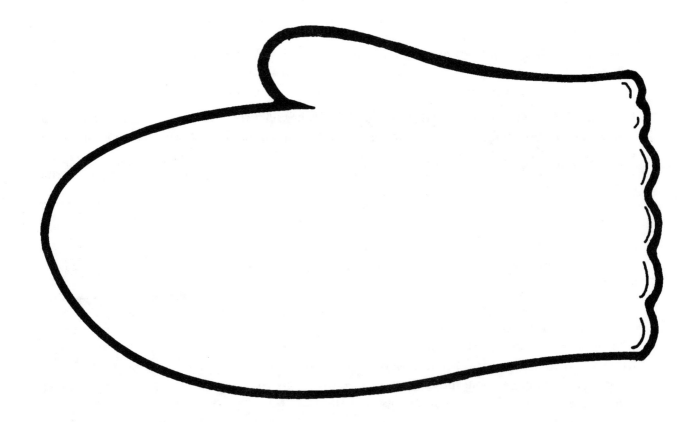

Three Little Kittens *(cont.)*

F,   find,   find   your   mit – tens.

Find   your   mit – tens you   naugh – ty   kit – tens!

Music Lesson

Skills

- differentiates between loud and soft
- recognizes the sound /f/
- knows the hand sign for the letter "f"

Materials

- collection of mittens for students to try on

Before the Lesson

1. Copy and enlarge the jingle for the letter "f" on this page onto butcher paper or chart paper.
2. Copy and enlarge the nursery rhyme "Three Little Kittens" from page 37 onto butcher paper or chart paper.

Procedure

1. Read the nursery rhyme "Three Little Kittens" to the class. Read the rhyme a second time, inviting the students to join in as you track the words on the chart.
2. Show students the chart of the jingle for the letter "f." Read the jingle to the class. Explain to the students that this jingle is similar to the nursery rhyme "Three Little Kittens," but that this one will help them to remember the sound that the letter "f" makes as in *find*. Say the jingle together, tracking the words on the chart as they are read.
3. Show the students the hand sign for the letter "f." (See example.) Explain that this is the sign that is used to represent the letter "f" for those who cannot hear or speak. This will also help them to remember "f" as they make this sign during the jingle. Say the jingle again, using the hand sign for "f" when "f" is read on the chart.
4. Explain that the next exercise they will do with this jingle will be a study in loud and soft. We will be using mittens, just like the three little kittens, to illustrate this. Choose a group of students to come to the front of the class and clap as they say the jingle. Choose another group of students to come to the front of the class and clap with mittens on their hands as they say the jingle. Which one clapped louder? Which clapped softer? Let students take turns clapping with and without the mittens.

Mary, Mary, Quite Contrary

Mary, Mary, quite contrary,

How does your garden grow?

With silver bells and cockle-shells,

And pretty maids all in a row.

Mary, Mary, Quite Contrary *(cont.)*

Art Lesson

Skills

- creates own musical instruments

Materials

- broken crayons, small pieces of wood, crayons, or small rolls of paper to use as "stoppers"
- flower pots (assorted sizes), one per student
- permanent markers or acrylic paint
- wooden sticks or plastic spoons, one per student
- butcher paper or chart paper
- containers for water
- paint or markers
- string

Before the Lesson

1. Copy or enlarge the nursery rhyme "Mary, Mary, Quite Contrary" (page 44) onto butcher paper or chart paper. Display it in the classroom.

2. Fill containers with water.

Procedure

1. Read the rhyme "Mary, Mary, Quite Contrary," using the enlarged version of the rhyme. Read the rhyme a second time, tracking the words, inviting students who feel comfortable joining in to do so.

2. Hold up a flower pot (previously decorated) and ask, What does a flowerpot have to do with this nursery rhyme? Take answers. This will help students make a thematic connection with the activity and the rhyme.

3. Explain that we are going to decorate the flower pots and then turn them into bells. Can anyone guess why we want to use different sizes of flowerpots? *(Larger pots will produce a different sound than the smaller pots.)*

4. Give students ample time to decorate their pots. (If necessary, let them dry overnight.)

5. Model for the students how to make the bell's "stopper." Tie the string around a piece of wood, broken crayon, or small roll of paper. The object should be larger than the hole in the pot.

Mary, Mary, Quite Contrary *(cont.)*

Art Lesson *(cont.)*

Procedure *(cont.)*

6. Thread the other end of the string through the inside of the pot. The "stopper" should hold the string to the inside, allowing the pot to hang down when held from the string.

7. Dangle the pot upside down, holding the string in one hand while you strike your bell with a wooden stick or plastic spoon.

8. After modeling the procedure of making the flower pot bells, lay out the supplies and allow students to begin.

9. Allow time to play the beautifully decorated bells and to compare tones.

46

Mary, Mary, Quite Contrary (cont.)

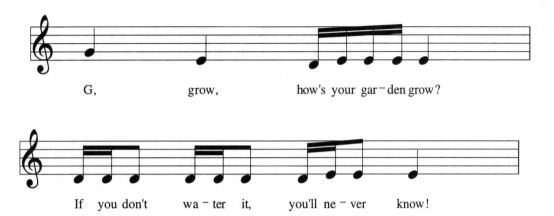

G,   grow,   how's your gar-den grow?

If you don't   wa-ter it,   you'll ne-ver   know!

Music Lesson

Skills

- notes differences in tone
- recognizes the sound /g/
- knows the hand sign for the letter "g"

Materials

- enlarged version of "Mary, Mary, Quite Contrary"
- enlarged version of letter "g" jingle
- flower pot bells from Art Lesson (page 45)
- small sticks or spoons
- chart paper
- markers

Procedure

1. Read the nursery rhyme "Mary, Mary, Quite Contrary" to the class, using the enlarged version. Reread the nursery rhyme, tracking the words as you read them, and inviting the students to recite it along with you if they wish.

2. Write the letter "g" on chart paper. Ask the students if they can identify the letter. Take answers. Explain that they are about to learn a version of the nursery rhyme "Mary, Mary, Quite Contrary" that will help them to remember the letter "g" and the sound that it makes. Mention that they get to use their flowerpot bells with this rhyme.

3. Show the students the chart depicting the music staff and the words to the letter "g" jingle. Recite the jingle to them, clapping the rhythm with your hands. Allow them to join in with you the second time, clapping the rhythm as they recite the jingle. If they seem to have trouble following the rhythm pattern, repeat as necessary.

Mary, Mary, Quite Contrary *(cont.)*

Music Lesson *(cont.)*

4. Pass out the flower pot bells and chime the rhythm on the bells by tapping the stick on the bell, using the same rhythm pattern used in step three. Allow students to try the pattern using their bells.

5. Once students are comfortable with their bells, have a parade or give a performance for another class.

6. Show the students the hand sign for the letter "g." (See example.) Explain that this is the sign that is used to represent the letter "g" for those who cannot hear or talk. This will also help them to remember the sound that the letter "g" makes in the word *garden* as they make this sign during the jingle. Read the jingle to the class. Sing the jingle together, tracking the words as they are read. Repeat the jingle, using the hand sign for "g" when "g" is read on the chart.

Pease Porridge Hot

Pease porridge hot,

Pease porridge cold,

Pease porridge in the pot

Nine days old.

Some like it hot,

Some like it cold,

Some like it in the pot

Nine days old!

Pease Porridge Hot *(cont.)*

Art Lesson

Skills

- experiments with patterns
- creates shapes
- experiments with space
- experiments with line
- experiments with color

Materials

- one piece of 8½" x 11" (22 cm x 28 cm) white drawing paper for each student
- markers

Before the Lesson

Copy and enlarge the nursery rhyme "Pease Porridge Hot" (page 49) onto butcher paper or chart paper. Display in the classroom.

Procedure

1. Read the nursery rhyme "Pease Porridge Hot" to the students using the enlarged version. Read the rhyme again, inviting the students to join in with you in tracking the words as you read.

2. Give each student a piece of white drawing paper. Explain that they are going to pretend that they spilled hot porridge all over their papers. Ask, How would you draw it? Model for the students as you draw a scribble of wild circles on your page.

3. Model for the students as you explain the process of making scribble art. Fill in each enclosed shape with either a pattern or a solid color using markers. Patterns could include stripes, polka dots, hearts, checkers, stars, etc.

4. Allow students to create their own scribbles.

5. Allow students to fill in their shapes with their own colors and patterns.

6. Display the scribble art in the classroom.

Pease Porridge Hot *(cont.)*

H,   hot,   pease   por-ridge hot!

What if   it's   cold?   I   hope   it's   not!

Music Lesson

Skills

- differentiates between loud and soft
- recognizes the sound /h/
- knows the hand sign for the letter "h"

Before the Lesson

1. Copy and enlarge the nursery rhyme "Pease Porridge Hot" (page 49) onto butcher paper.
2. Copy and enlarge the jingle for "h" onto butcher paper or chart paper.

Procedure

1. Read the nursery rhyme "Pease Porridge Hot" to the class. Read the rhyme a second time, inviting the students to join in as you track the words on the chart.

2. Show students the chart of the jingle for the letter "h." Read the jingle to the class. Explain to the students that this jingle is similar to the nursery rhyme "Pease Porridge Hot" but that this one will help them to remember the sound that the letter "h" makes as in *hot*. Say the jingle together, tracking the words on the chart as they are read.

3. Show the students the hand sign for the letter "h." (See example.) Explain that this is the sign that is used to represent the letter "h" for those who cannot hear or talk. This will also help them to remember "h" as they make this sign during the jingle. Say the jingle again, using the hand sign for "h" when "h" is read on the chart.

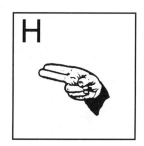

4. Explain that the next exercise they will do with this jingle will be a clapping game.

Pease Porridge Hot (cont.)

Music Lesson (cont.)

Procedure (cont.)

5. Tell students to choose a partner and sit on the floor facing his or her partner with legs crossed. Model for the students the following clapping game with the jingle:

H	(do hand-sign for "h")
Hot	(do hand-sign for "h" again)
Pease	(slap both hands down on thighs)
Porridge	(clap hands together)
Hot	(clap right hand to your partner's right hand)
What	(clap hands together again)
If it's	(clap left hand to your partner's left hand)
Cold	(clap hands together again)
I	(slap both hands down on thighs)
Hope	(clap hands together again)
It's	(clap both hands with partner's hands at the same time)
Not	(clap both hands with partner's hands again)

6. Repeat as many times as necessary. Allow students to have fun with it while reinforcing the letter "h" and keeping the beat with their hands.

Little Jack Horner

Little Jack Horner

Sat in a corner,

Eating a Christmas pie.

He put in his thumb,

And pulled out a plum,

And said,

What a good boy am I!

Little Jack Horner (cont.)

Art Lesson 1

Skills

- identifies the color purple
- identifies the colors that make up the color purple
- uses color in an intuitive manner to express self
- produces a texture by pressing
- understands simple printmaking processes
- creates original prints

Materials

- clay (enough for each child to have a ball about the size of a golf ball)
- pie tins, at least two per table
- red, white, and blue tempera paint
- Color Wheel (page 56)
- a plum

Before the Lesson

1. Copy and enlarge the nursery rhyme "Little Jack Horner" from page 53 onto chart paper or enlarge it so that the class can see the words easily.

2. Mix two different tints of purple for every two pie tins. (Use more red than blue in one tin and more blue than red in the other tin.) Leave one pie tin empty for demonstration purposes.

3. Copy, enlarge, and color the color wheel from page 56.

Procedure

1. Read the nursery rhyme "Little Jack Horner" to the class, using the large display version. Read the rhyme again, tracking the words and allowing the class to join in if they are familiar with the rhyme.

2. Reenact the nursery rhyme using one of the pie tins and a chunk of clay in the shape of a ball. Stick your thumb into the clay and pull it out of the pie tin. Discuss with the students that a plum is a fruit that grows on trees. Many people use the word *plum* to refer to a color. Hold up a plum. Ask, What color is this plum? (*purple*) Explain that this is the color that people refer to when they say that something is *plum-colored*. The two colors that go together to make this color are red and blue.

Little Jack Horner (cont.)

Art Lesson 1 (cont.)

Procedure (cont.)

3. Demonstrate the mixing of red and blue by putting a dab of red tempera paint and a dab of blue tempera paint into one of the pie tins. Notice that the plum color that was created is very dark. What color would lighten it up to the plum color that we need? How about adding the color white? Add a dab of white paint and show the color that appears when all three colors are mixed together.

4. Red, yellow, and blue are called *primary colors*. Yellow and red make orange, yellow and blue make green, and red and blue make purple. Orange, green, and purple are called *secondary colors*. Notice that on the color wheel each secondary color is placed midway between the two primary colors that produce it. Colors directly opposite each other on the color wheel are called *complementary colors*—red and green, orange and blue, and yellow and purple.

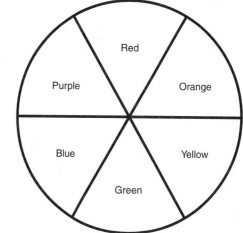

5. Give each child a ball of clay. Allow him or her to play with it and reenact the nursery rhyme together with the pretend plum.

6. Explain that the clay that they have will be used as a stamp. They can shape the stamp any way that they wish. Pressing the clay onto the table before dabbing it into the paint will create the flat surface needed to get a nicely shaped print onto the paper.

7. Demonstrate some ideas for shapes to make with the clay.

8. Distribute a couple of pie tins to each table with a different tint of plum color in each one.

9. Let the students have a great time experimenting with their self-made stamps. This activity, using Jack's pie tin, a pretend plum, and "plum-colored" paint should be a big hit!

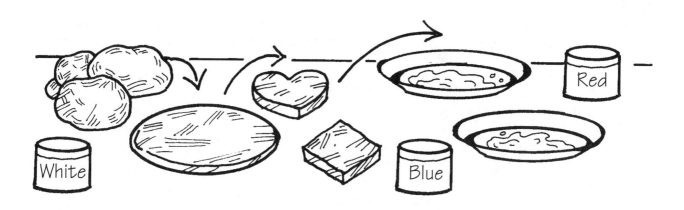

Little Jack Horner *(cont.)*

Color Wheel

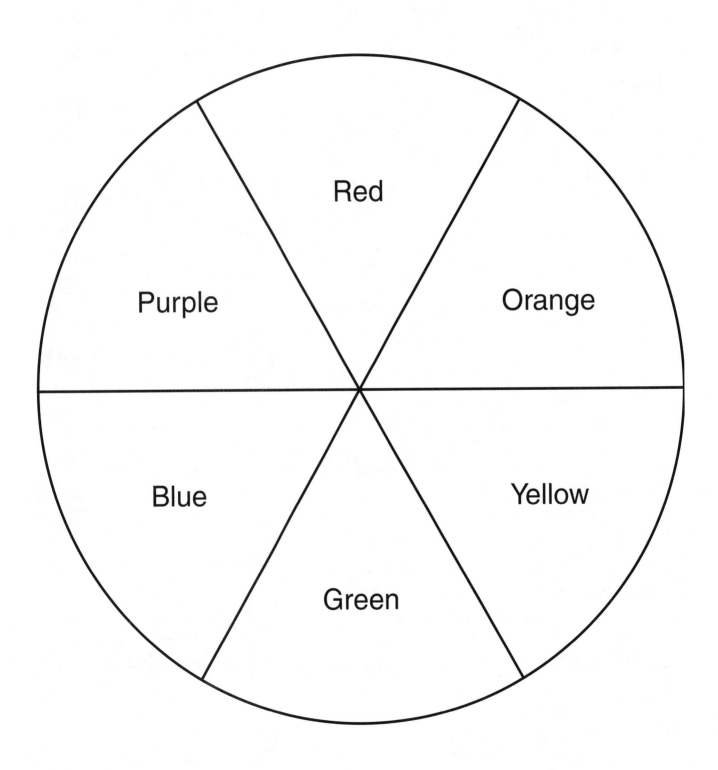

Little Jack Horner (cont.)

Art Lesson 2

Skills

- creates an art form using a sculptural process that enables creative three-dimensional expressions
- designs a three-dimensional object

Materials

- copy of the nursery rhyme "Little Jack Horner" on chart paper used in Art Lesson 1
- container of cinnamon with a sprinkle top
- miniature pie tins (1 per student)
- flour
- oil
- salt
- water
- potpourri or other scent oil
- craft sticks, one per student
- clear acrylic sealer spray
- cotton balls
- chart paper
- wax paper
- large bowl

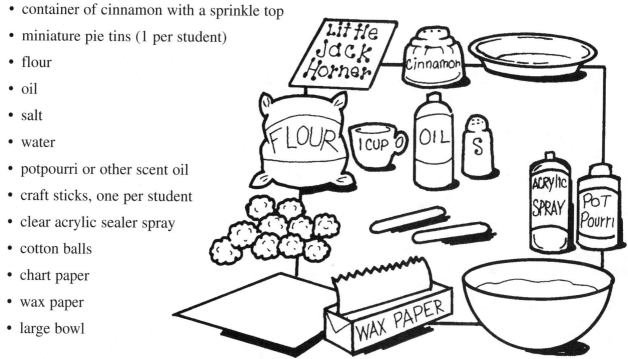

Before the Lesson

1. Cut enough sheets of wax paper so that each student has a 12" (30 cm) square piece.
2. Lay the wax paper at each child's work area and sprinkle flour on it.
3. Put a craft stick at each child's workspace.
4. Put five large cotton balls at each child's workspace.
5. In a large bowl, mix 2 cups (450 g) flour, ¼ cup (60 mL) oil, ½ cup (100 g) salt, and ½ cup (120 mL) water together with your hands until dough forms. Repeat this process as many times as needed to create enough dough for the entire class to have a baseball-sized ball of dough.

Procedure

1. Read the nursery rhyme "Little Jack Horner," using the enlarged version of the rhyme from Art Lesson 1, page 54. Read the rhyme a second time, tracking the words. Invite the students to join in if they know the words.

Little Jack Horner *(cont.)*

Art Lesson 2 *(cont.)*

Procedure *(cont.)*

2. Discuss with the students how smells make them feel and allow students to discuss smells that they feel are good smells and smells that they feel are bad smells. Chart these suggestions.

3. Ask, Do you think the scent of freshly baked pie is a good smell or a bad smell? How does it make you feel when you see a freshly baked pie cooling on the stove? Take answers.

4. Explain to the students that today they will be making a craft that will radiate nice smells. It will look like a pie, but it will not be edible. It will be a decoration used as a room freshener.

Making the "Pie"

1. Sprinkle a small amount of flour on the wax paper and lay your ball of dough on the wax paper. Knead it until it is like play dough. Press it out flat like a pancake.

2. Wash your hands.

3. Place large cotton balls in the pie tin until the bottom of the tin is completely covered. (This is the "fruit" of the pie.)

4. Allow the teacher to sprinkle potpourri oil onto the cotton balls.

5. Place the dough (pie crust) over the cotton balls and seal (pinch) around the sides of the pie tin like a real pie.

6. Sprinkle cinnamon over the top.

7. Cut slits around the circular center of the pie with a craft stick.

8. Spray acrylic sealant over the top of the pies.

Teacher Safety Note: Spray the clear acrylic sealer outside the room to avoid inhalation of fumes.

I,   I,   what a good boy am I,   said

Lit - tle Jack   Hor - ner with a thumb in his pie!

Music Lesson

Skills

- makes own musical instruments
- recognizes the sound /i/
- maintains a steady beat
- knows the hand sign for the letter "i"

Materials

- small aluminum pie pans, one per student
- butcher paper or chart paper
- streamers (three colors)
- tape
- copy of "Little Jack Horner" (page 53)

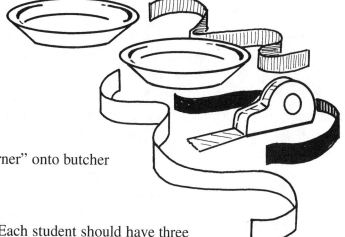

Before the Lesson

1. Enlarge the nursery rhyme "Little Jack Horner" onto butcher paper or chart paper.

2. Enlarge the jingle for the letter "i."

3. Cut the streamers into 24" (61 cm) strips. Each student should have three streamers of different colors.

Procedure

1. Read the nursery rhyme "Little Jack Horner," using the enlarged version. Reread the rhyme, tracking the words as you read them and allowing students to join in if they feel comfortable.

2. Hold up a pie pan and ask, What does a pie pan have to do with this nursery rhyme? Does the rhyme mention a pie? What kind of pie is mentioned?

3. Explain that today they will make a tambourine-like instrument with a pie pan for use with another version of this nursery rhyme.

Little Jack Horner *(cont.)*

Music Lesson *(cont.)*

Procedure

4. Model for the students how to tape the three 24" (61 cm) streamers to the pie pan. Give each student a pie pan, three pieces of tape, and three streamers to do the same.

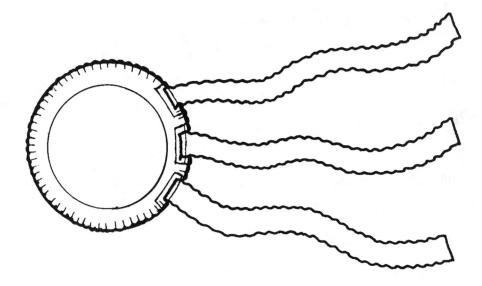

5. Read the enlarged version of the letter "i" jingle. Read it again, clapping the beat as you say it. Explain to the students that the next time you read it, they are going to use their tambourines to tap the beat on the backside of the pie plate. Model for the students the proper way to keep the beat with the tambourine. Allow the students to try it. Encourage the students to march around so that the streamers will move.

6. Show the students the hand sign for the letter "i." (See example.) Explain that this is the sign that is used to represent the letter "i" for those who cannot hear or speak. This will also help them to remember "i" as they make this sign during the jingle. Say the jingle again, using the hand sign for "i" when "i" is read on the chart.

Diddle, Diddle, Dumpling

Diddle, diddle, dumpling,

My son John

Went to bed with his

Trousers on;

One shoe off,

The other shoe on,

Diddle, diddle, dumpling

My son John.

Diddle, Diddle, Dumpling *(cont.)*

Art Lesson

Skills

- creates patterns from texture
- creates shapes
- recognizes negative space
- recognizes patterns
- colors

Materials

- 8½" x 11" (22 cm x 28 cm) white paper, one per student
- shoes with tread patterns underneath
- colored chalk
- pencils, one per student
- crayons

Before the Lesson

Copy and enlarge the nursery rhyme "Diddle, Diddle, Dumpling" from page 61 onto chart paper or butcher paper and display in the classroom.

Procedure

1. Read the nursery rhyme "Diddle, Diddle, Dumpling" to the class, using the enlarged version. Reread the rhyme, tracking the words as you read them and inviting students to join in with you.

2. Tie in the story with the activity by discussing the rhyme. Explain that maybe Diddle Dumpling John had one shoe on because he loved to do this activity so much!

3. Model for the students steps 4–8 and then let them try it themselves.

4. Draw a large shape on the white paper with a pencil. Try to fill the page. The shape could be a heart, a house, a flower, etc.

5. Look at the bottom of your shoe. Does it have interesting tread marks on it? Are there patterns of lines or shapes? If so, you are in luck. If not, ask a friend if he or she will help you with the next part of this activity.

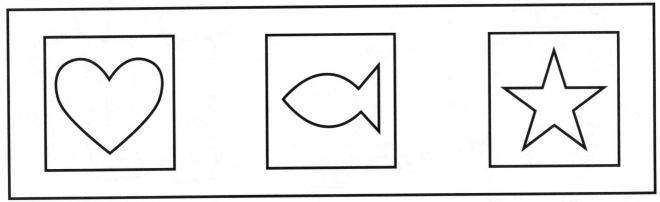

Diddle, Diddle, Dumpling (cont.)

Art Lesson (cont.)

Procedure (cont.)

6. Rub a piece of colored chalk across the tread marks on the bottom of the shoe until it is completely covered with chalk. Press the shoe onto the white paper creating a print of the tread marks on the shape (outline) that you have drawn. If the marks do not fill in the entire shape, chalk the shoe and press it on again. Marks outside of the shape will be covered up later, so disregard those.

7. Trace over the shape with a dark crayon. Trace the tread prints inside of the shape with your crayon.

8. Color all of the *negative space*, the space around your shape, with a dark color so that all of the extra chalk tread prints are covered, as well as the white paper.

9. Use different colors of crayons to color in the shapes or line patterns inside of your shape.

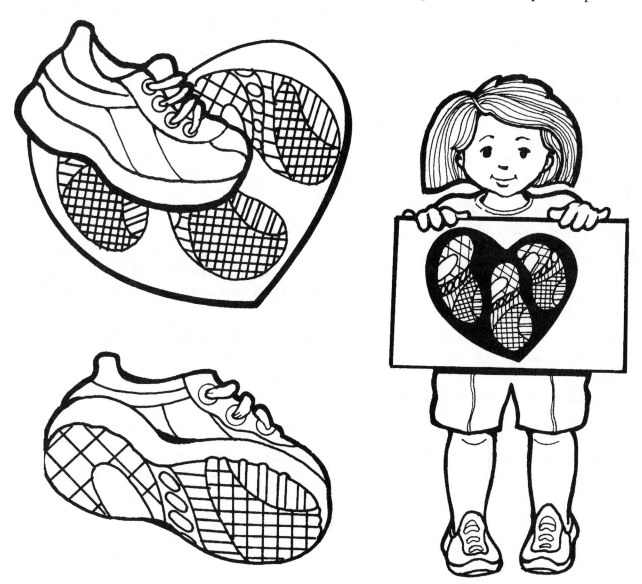

Diddle, Diddle, Dumpling *(cont.)*

J,   John,   Little Dum - pling John   had

one   shoe   off   and   one   shoe   on!

Music Lesson

Skills

- recognizes the sound /j/
- keeps rhythm with feet

- knows the hand sign for the letter "j"

Before the Lesson

1. Copy and enlarge the jingle for the letter "j" onto butcher paper or chart paper.

2. Copy and enlarge the nursery rhyme, "Diddle, Diddle, Dumpling" from page 61 onto butcher paper or chart paper.

Procedure

1. Read the nursery rhyme "Diddle, Diddle, Dumpling" to the class. Read the rhyme a second time, inviting the students to join in as you track the words on the chart.

2. Show students the chart of the jingle for the letter "j." Read the jingle to the class. Explain to the students that this jingle is similar to the nursery rhyme "Diddle, Diddle, Dumpling" but that this one will help them to remember the sound that the letter "j" makes as in *John*. Say the jingle together, tracking the words on the chart as they are read.

3. Show the students the hand sign for the letter "j." (See example.) Explain that this is the sign that is used to represent the letter "j" for those who cannot hear or talk. This will also help them to remember "j" as they make this sign during the jingle. Repeat the jingle, using the hand sign for "j" when "j" is read on the chart.

4. Explain that the next exercise they will do with this jingle will be a game that will require them to keep the beat with their feet since Little Dumpling John probably liked to take his shoes off to dance!

5. Form a large circle. Turn to the right and walk in a circle while saying the jingle for "j." Take a step on each beat. After reciting the jingle, change the way you keep the beat around the circle by hopping on the right foot until the entire jingle is over, then hopping on the left foot, and finally hopping on both feet.

Georgie Porgie

Georgie Porgie

Pudding and pie,

Kissed the girls

And made them cry;

When the boys

Came out to play,

Georgie Porgie

Ran away.

Georgie Porgie *(cont.)*

Art Lesson

Skills

- manipulates and experiments with paint (pudding)
- experiments with texture
- uses own symbols to communicate thoughts and feelings

Materials

- large white sheets of paper, two per student
- chocolate pudding
- paper plates, one per student
- wet towels or napkins for cleaning

Before the Lesson

1. Copy and enlarge the nursery rhyme "Georgie Porgie" (page 65) onto butcher paper or chart paper. Display it in the classroom.

2. Have students wash their hands thoroughly.

Procedure

1. Read the enlarged version of the rhyme "Georgie Porgie." Read the rhyme again, tracking the words as they are read and encouraging students to recite the rhyme along with you.

2. Ask, What does Georgie Porgie like to eat? *(pudding and pie)* Explain that today they will be like Georgie Porgie as they paint with chocolate pudding, and just like Georgie Porgie, they can lick their fingers when they're finished!

3. Model for the students the finger painting process by dipping your fingers into the chocolate pudding and creating shapes on the paper. Explain to the students that they will each have one sheet of paper on which to experiment, and another sheet on which to draw a picture.

4. Put some pudding on a paper plate for each student.

5. Let the students dig in, using their practice sheets, feeling the texture of the pudding on their fingers as they create shapes and figures on their papers.

6. When the students are finished with their practice sheets, hang or lay them out to dry and hand out more sheets with which to create. Encourage students to use a free form style and enjoy the process rather than worrying about the product on this assignment.

7. Allow the students to lick their fingers (if the wish) when they are finished and use wet towels to finish cleaning their hands and work area.

Georgie Porgie *(cont.)*

K,   kiss,   Geor-gie pud-din' and   pie!

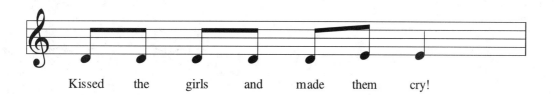

Kissed   the   girls   and   made   them   cry!

Music Lesson

Skills

- recognizes the sound /k/
- knows the hand sign for the letter "k"
- understands the importance of clarity when singing

Materials

- tongue depressors, one per student
- butcher paper and chart paper

Before the Lesson

1. Copy and enlarge the jingle for the letter "k" onto butcher paper or chart paper.
2. Copy and enlarge the nursery rhyme "Georgie Porgie" from page 65 onto butcher paper or chart paper.

Procedure

1. Read the nursery rhyme "Georgie Porgie" to the class. Read the rhyme a second time, inviting the students to join in as you track the words on the chart.

2. Show students the chart of the jingle for the letter "k." Read the rhyme to the class. Explain to the students that this jingle is similar to the nursery rhyme "Georgie Porgie" but that this one will help them to remember the sound that the letter "k" makes as in *kiss*. Say the jingle together, tracking the words on the chart as they are read.

   ![K hand sign]

3. Show the students the hand sign for the letter "k." (See example.) Explain that this is the sign that is used to represent the letter "k" for those who cannot hear or speak. This will also help them to remember "k" as they make this sign during the jingle. Repeat the jingle, using the hand sign for "k" when "k" is read on the chart.

4. Ask, Why do you think it is important that a singer not chew gum or have anything in his or her mouth while singing? Take answers. Say, Imagine Georgie Porgie was singing to you, and he had his mouth full of pudding and pie. How do you think it might sound? What should he do so that we could hear his singing voice more clearly? Give each student a tongue depressor. Explain that they are going to sing the jingle for the letter "k," but that they are going to hold a tongue depressor on their tongues as they sing it. Ask, What happened? Was it hard to sing in your best voice? Have students try it again without the tongue depressor. Discuss the differences in voice quality.

Mary Had a Little Lamb

Mary had a little lamb,

Its fleece was white as snow;

And everywhere that Mary went

The lamb was sure to go.

It followed her to school one day,

It was against the rule.

It made the students laugh and play,

To see a lamb at school.

Mary Had a Little Lamb *(cont.)*

Art Lesson

Skills

- recognizes colors
- uses crayons to create soft texture

Materials

- crayons
- copies of sentence strips (page 71)
- cotton balls
- white construction paper
- "How to Draw a Lamb" (page 70)
- butcher paper

Before the Lesson

1. Copy and enlarge the nursery rhyme "Mary Had a Little Lamb" from page 68 onto butcher paper or chart paper and display in the classroom.

2. Copy and enlarge the "How to Draw a Lamb" page onto butcher paper or chart paper.

3. Copy the sentence strips from page 71 so that each student has one sentence strip.

Procedure

1. Read the nursery rhyme "Mary Had a Little Lamb" to the class using the enlarged version. Reread the nursery rhyme, inviting the students to say it along with you and track the words.

2. Discuss the nursery rhyme. Ask, Has anyone ever touched a lamb before? What does it feel like? *Texture* is the quality of a surface. How could we draw a lamb to make it look like it has the texture that you described? Give each student a cotton ball. Have students feel the texture of the cotton ball and compare it to the way they think a lamb would feel. Suggest trying to create the same textured feel on the lamb, using a cotton ball.

3. Model for the students as you use the "How to Draw a Lamb" page to draw a lamb onto a large piece of white butcher paper. Attach the first sentence strip, Mary had a little lamb, her fleece was black as _____.

4. Explain that they will each get a sentence strip that will designate the color of their lambs and also a space that they will be able to fill in as a comparative. What could they write in the blank that would fit the description of something that is always black? (*darkness, ink, coal*)

5. Since the lamb is supposed to be black, explain that they are going to try to create the texture of curly lamb's wool by taking the paper off of an old broken crayon. They will then rub the crayon on its side in a circular motion as they fill in the body of the lamb. This will create a soft, textured look. Model this procedure for the students.

6. Go over the other sentence strips so that the students get an idea of what they need to do.

7. Give each student a piece of paper and a sentence strip. Read the strips aloud as they are handed out. Each student will do only one drawing with one sentence strip.

8. When all students are finished, share the colorful lambs in a sharing circle, allowing the students to read what they came up with for each color.

Mary Had a Little Lamb (cont.)

How to Draw a Lamb

1.

2.

3.

4.

5.

6.

Mary Had a Little Lamb (cont.)

Sentence Strips

Mary had a little lamb, her fleece was black as _____.

Mary had a little lamb, her fleece was red as _____.

Mary had a little lamb, her fleece was blue as _____.

Mary had a little lamb, her fleece was yellow as _____.

Mary had a little lamb, her fleece was green as _____.

Mary had a little lamb, her fleece was orange as _____.

Mary had a little lamb, her fleece was purple as _____.

Mary had a little lamb, her fleece was brown as _____.

Mary had a little lamb, her fleece was pink as _____.

Mary Had a Little Lamb *(cont.)*

L,   lamb,   Ma — ry's lamb,

fol-lowed her   to school,   she's   in   a   jam!

Music Lesson

Skills

- recognizes the sound /l/
- follows a beat pattern
- knows the hand sign for the letter "l"

Materials

- drum
- butcher paper or chart paper

Before the Lesson

1. Copy and enlarge the jingle for the letter "l" on this page onto butcher paper or chart paper.
2. Copy and enlarge the nursery rhyme "Mary Had a Little Lamb" from page 68 onto butcher paper or chart paper.

Procedure

1. Read the nursery rhyme "Mary Had a Little Lamb" to the class. Read the jingle a second time, inviting the students to join in as you track the words on the chart.
2. Show students the chart of the jingle for the letter "l." Read the rhyme to the class. Explain to the students that this jingle is similar to the nursery rhyme "Mary Had a Little Lamb," but that this one will help them to remember the sound that the letter "l" makes as in *lamb*. Repeat the jingle, tracking the words on the chart as they are read.
3. Show the students the hand sign for the letter "l." (See example.) Explain that this is the sign that is used to represent the letter "l" for those who cannot hear or talk. This will also help them to remember "l" as they make this sign during the jingle. Repeat the jingle, using the hand sign for "l" when "l" is read on the chart.
4. Explain that Mary's lamb followed her to school one day, which was against the rule. Say, We are going to play a follow the leader game that is not against the rule. We will choose one person to be the lamb (leader). The lamb will decide if the beat for the jingle will be fast or slow. He or she will keep this steady beat on the drum. *If the beat is fast, the class will sing the jingle fast. If the beat is slow, the class will sing the jingle slowly.* Let as many students be the "lamb" as time allows.

Little Miss Muffet

Little Miss Muffet

Sat on a tuffet

Eating her curds and whey.

Along came a spider,

Who sat down beside her,

And frightened

Miss Muffet away.

 #3011 Teaching Art and Music

Little Miss Muffet *(cont.)*

Art Lesson 1

Skills

- manipulates and experiments with paint
- recognizes and reproduces lines
- uses straight lines
- uses curved lines
- learns that lines can be used to enclose space and define shape, express emotions, and illustrate ideas or objects

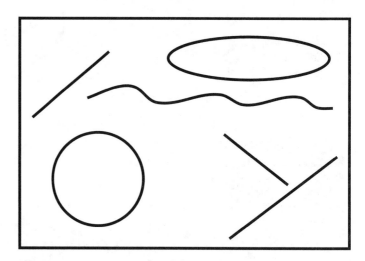

Materials

- 12" x 18" (30 cm x 46 cm) black construction paper, one per student
- copy of "Little Miss Muffet" nursery rhyme (page 73)
- drinking straws, one per student
- "How to Draw a Spider" (page 76)
- Spider Identification Cards (page 77)
- butcher paper or chart paper
- pencils, one per student
- white tempera paint
- paintbrushes
- masking tape
- paper

Before the Lesson

1. Copy and enlarge the nursery rhyme "Little Miss Muffet" (page 73) onto butcher paper or chart paper.
2. Copy the Spider Identification Cards from page 77 and cut them apart.
3. Tape a piece of black construction paper onto a flat workspace for each student.

Procedure

1. Read the nursery rhyme "Little Miss Muffet," using the enlarged version on chart paper. Track the words as you read them the second time so students may join in if they already know the words.
2. Discuss different types of spiders that students already know about. Discuss the sizes of spiders and how different their legs make them look. Use the different spider examples to illustrate to students how some spiders have legs so thin that they look like threads (daddy long legs) and others have legs that look hairy and thick (tarantulas).

Little Miss Muffet (cont.)

Art Lesson 1 *(cont.)*

Procedure *(cont.)*

3. After observing and discussing different spiders, explain to the students that in order to draw spiders as they see them, they need to understand what a *line* is.

4. Have each student get a pencil and a piece of scratch paper on which to practice making lines. Begin by asking the students to slowly draw a straight, dark line. Underneath it, ask them to quickly draw a straight line. Discuss the differences in the lines that were made. Ask, Why did the speed make a difference?

5. Continue studying lines by asking the students to draw a curvy line slowly and another one quickly. Ask them if they can make a *thick* line and a *thin* line. Have them write their names, first slowly and then quickly. Ask, What happens to the lines in the signature? Discuss.

6. Explain to the students that they are going to learn how to draw a spider. Give each student a new piece of paper. Follow the procedure for "How To Draw a Spider" (page 76) so that all of the students are doing it together. After the drawings are finished, explain that the spider's appearance can be individualized by changing the thickness of the lines on the legs, by adding hair-like lines on the legs and body, or by coloring it.

7. Explain to students that when they draw a line that surrounds a shape, like when drawing the spider, they are making a descriptive line called an *outline*.

8. We are going to experiment further with line using white paint and black paper.

9. Model for the students how to create lines with tempera paint by blowing a spot of white tempera paint to the edge of the taped-down black paper with a drinking straw. Show them how to blow the paint to the edges of the paper, forming thick, thin, straight, and curvy lines. Remind the students to blow air out and not to inhale. The straw should not touch the paper at any time.

10. Go to each student's work area and drop a spot of white tempera paint onto the center of the black construction paper with a paintbrush. Do not touch the paintbrush to the paper.

11. Give each student a drinking straw to begin blowing the paint around.

12. Let the paint dry before removing the tape. When they are displayed, they will look like spider webs hanging above Miss Muffet's head!

Little Miss Muffet (cont.)

How to Draw a Spider

1. Make the spider's head. 	2. Add a face. 
3. Add a body. 	4. Add spinnerets. 
5. Add four legs to one side. 	6. Add four more legs. 

Little Miss Muffet (cont.)

Spider Identification Cards

Golden Silk Spider

Garden Spider

Fisher Spider

Tarantula

Little Miss Muffet *(cont.)*

Art Lesson 2

Skills

- uses colors in an inventive manner to express self
- able to identify primary and secondary colors by name
- uses curved lines
- uses straight lines

Materials

- 12" x 18" (30 cm x 46 cm) white construction paper, one per student
- enlarged copy of "Little Miss Muffet" nursery rhyme from Art Lesson 1
- Color Mixing work sheet (page 79), one per student
- red, blue, and yellow tempera paint
- drinking straws, one per student
- enlarged color wheel (page 56)
- 3 paint brushes
- masking tape

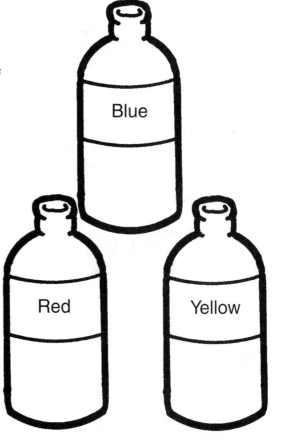

Before the Lesson

1. Tape a piece of white construction paper onto a flat workspace for each student.
2. Copy the color wheel onto chart paper and color it.
3. Copy the Color Mixing work sheet for each student.

Procedure

1. Review the nursery rhyme "Little Miss Muffet" by reading it to the class, using the chart made in Art Lesson 1 to track the words as they are read. Allow students to join in reading the rhyme if they feel comfortable doing so.
2. Review the new terminology learned in Art Lesson 1 by asking questions about lines. (*Lines, the recorded action of a child's drawing or other linear design process, can enclose space and define shape, express emotions, and illustrate ideas or objects.*) Ask, How can lines be changed? What are some different types of lines?
3. Explain that today they will continue to work with lines in the same way, but they will make some new discoveries along the way. They will be working with the *primary colors*—red, yellow, and blue. They will again blow the paint across the paper, creating lines. However, they will add colors as they go, creating *secondary colors*—green, orange, and purple.
4. Begin by dropping a spot of yellow paint onto each student's white paper. Hand out straws to each student and allow the students a few minutes to blow the paint around on their papers. Then go around the room again, dropping a red spot of paint on each student's paper, close to but not touching the yellow spot.

Little Miss Muffet *(cont.)*

Art Lesson 2 *(cont.)*

Procedure *(cont.)*

5. Allow the students to blow the red spot around on the paper, blending the colors red and yellow. Ask the students what happens when the red and the yellow paint overlap. If they answer that the paint turns orange, they are correct and have created their first secondary color. Remind them that they have mixed red and yellow to create orange.

6. Add a spot of blue paint to each student's paper. See if they can discover what the final two secondary colors are. Discuss which colors created green and which colors created purple. Remind them that red and blue make purple and yellow and blue make green. Have the children fill in the answers to the work sheet below.

7. Show them the enlarged version of the color wheel from page 56. Point out how the primary colors form a triangle and how each of the secondary colors finds its place between the two colors that created it. They will love their colorful webs which turn out looking like different colors of spiders all over their page! Miss Muffet would definitely get off of her tuffet to do this fun activity!

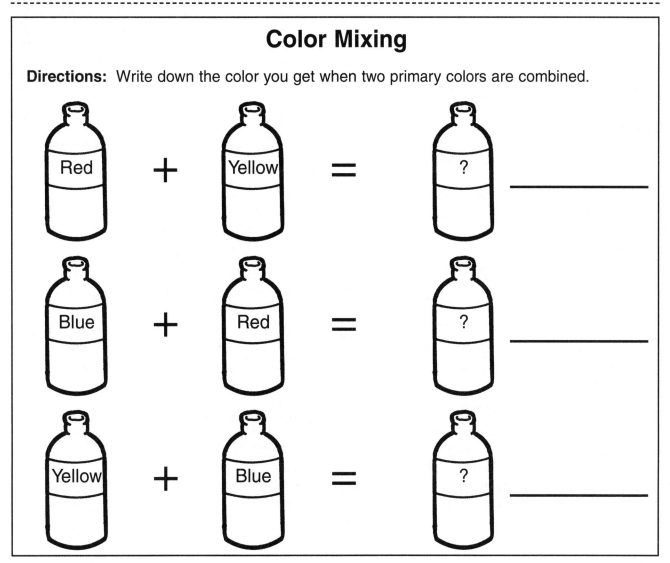

Color Mixing

Directions: Write down the color you get when two primary colors are combined.

Little Miss Muffet (cont.)

M,   Muf – fet,   Lit – tle   Miss!

Would   not   give   that   spi – der   a   kiss!

Music Lesson

Skills

- recognizes the sound /m/
- knows the hand sign for the letter "m"
- differentiates between loud and soft sounds

Materials

- bean bag spider or large plastic spider
- butcher paper or chart paper

Before the Lesson

1. Copy and enlarge the jingle for the letter "m" onto butcher paper or chart paper.

2. Copy and enlarge the nursery rhyme "Little Miss Muffet" from page 73 onto butcher paper or chart paper.

Procedure

1. Read the nursery rhyme "Little Miss Muffet" to the class. Read the rhyme a second time, inviting the students to join in as you track the words on the chart.

2. Show students the chart of the jingle for the letter "m." Read the jingle to the class. Explain to the students that this jingle is similar to the nursery rhyme "Little Miss Muffet" but that this one will help them to remember the sound that the letter "m" makes as in *muffet*. Say the jingle together, tracking the words on the chart as they are read.

3. Show students the hand sign for the letter "m." (See example.) Explain that this is the sign that is used to represent the letter "m" for those who cannot hear or talk. This will also help them to remember "m" as they make this sign during the jingle. Say the jingle again, using the hand sign for "m" when "m" is read on the chart.

Little Miss Muffet *(cont.)*

Music Lesson *(cont.)*

Procedure *(cont.)*

4. Show students a toy spider. Explain that they are going to practice the skill of making their voices louder and softer through a hide and seek game with the spider. Repeat the rhyme softly and in a loud voice with the students.

5. Place the spider on a chair or in a place where students can see it. Explain to the students that as the seeker gets closer to where the spider is hidden, they will sing the rhyme louder and as he or she walks farther away, the singing will become softer. This will give the seeker hints as to where the spider is hidden.

6. Choose a student to go outside of the room while the spider is being hidden. After it is hidden, invite the student back into the room and begin singing the jingle for the letter "m."

7. Hide the spider and repeat as many times as desired giving other students an opportunity to find the spider.

Little Nut Tree

I had a little nut tree

Nothing would it bear

But a silver nutmeg

And a golden pear;

The King of Spain's daughter

Came to visit me,

And all was because

Of my little nut tree.

I skipped over water

I danced over sea

And all the birds in the air

Didn't catch me.

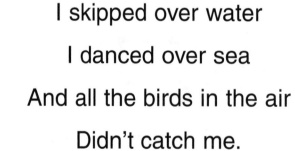

Little Nut Tree (cont.)

Art Lesson

Skills

- recognizes and reproduces lines
- uses his or her own symbols to communicate thoughts and feelings
- manipulates and experiments with paint to create a scribble that resembles objects in the immediate environment
- manipulates and experiments with paint using unconventional objects

Materials

- small amount of black tempera paint for each student in a small cup or on a small paper plate
- 8 ½ x 11" (22 cm x 28 cm) or 12" x 18" (30 cm x 46 cm) white paper, one per student
- sticks or small branches from a tree, one per student

Before the Lesson

Copy and enlarge the rhyme "Little Nut Tree" (page 82) onto chart paper or butcher paper and display in the classroom.

Procedure

1. Read the nursery rhyme "Little Nut Tree" to the class, using the large version prepared on chart paper. Read the rhyme again and invite the students to read it with you while you track the words on the chart.

2. Ask, What are some different tools that we use to create art? Take answers. Ask, Have you ever thought of using tools such as sticks to create art? Students will pretend that they are using branches from the little nut tree to create a piece of art.

3. Take students outside to each find a stick that they think would make a good painting tool. Encourage them to break off extra pieces of bark that may get in the way as they paint.

4. Model for the students as you dip your stick into the paint and apply it to the paper. Try to create a tree like the nut tree.

5. Allow students to experiment with their new art tools on their own papers.

6. Allow students to share their work with their peers, encouraging them to share any special techniques that they may have learned as they took part in the experiment. Brainstorm any other unusual objects that could be used to create art.

Little Nut Tree (cont.)

N,   nut – meg,   nut – meg and   pear

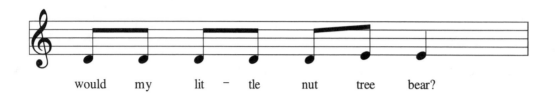

would   my   lit – tle   nut   tree   bear?

Music Lesson

Skills

- maintains a steady beat
- differentiates between a fast beat and a slow beat
- recognizes the sound /n/
- knows the hand sign for the letter "n"

Materials

- 12" (30 cm) tree branches, two per student
- butcher paper or chart paper

Before the Lesson

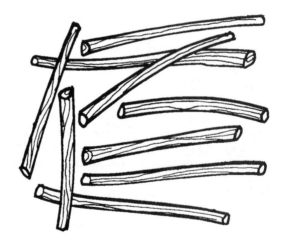

1. Copy and enlarge the rhyme "Little Nut Tree" (page 82) onto chart paper or butcher paper and display in the classroom.

2. Collect two tree branches per student to use as rhythm sticks if time doesn't permit students to find their own sticks during the lesson.

3. Copy and enlarge the jingle for the letter "n."

Procedure

1. Read the nursery rhyme "Little Nut Tree" to the class using the enlarged version created before the lesson. Reread the nursery rhyme, encouraging the students who feel comfortable with the rhyme to join in while you track the words on the chart.

2. Show students the chart of the jingle for the letter "n." Read the jingle to the class. Explain to the students that this jingle is similar to the nursery rhyme "Little Nut Tree" but that this one will help them to remember the sound that the letter "n" makes as in *nut*. Sing the jingle together, tracking the words on the chart as they are read.

Little Nut Tree (cont.)

Music Lesson (cont.)

Procedure (cont.)

3. Show students the hand sign for the letter "n." (See example.) Explain that this is the sign that is used to represent the letter "n" for those who cannot hear or talk. This will also help them to remember "n" as they make this sign during the jingle. Sing the jingle again, using the hand sign for "n" when "n" is read on the chart.

4. Ask, What do nut trees have that can help us make noise? (*branches*) Students will be making rhythm sticks. Rhythm sticks are used to keep the rhythm of a song. Students will use these tree parts to keep the rhythm to the tune of the jingle.

5. If time permits, take students outside to find two sticks each to use as rhythm sticks. If sticks are not readily available, you may want to collect them before the lesson.

6. After returning to the gathering area, play a short rhythm.

Have students play the rhythm back to you with their sticks. Explain that this is a steady beat.

Play the following rhythm:

Have students play the rhythm back to you with their sticks. Explain that this is not a steady beat.

7. Explain that next, they will play a game. Each time that a rhythm pattern is played with the rhythm sticks, the students will repeat the pattern with their sticks.

8. When finished, the students will hold the sticks straight side-by-side if it was a steady beat and cross them in an X if it was not a steady beat.

9. Introduce the musical version of "Little Nut Tree" using the tune from page 84. Sing each line to the students, giving them time to repeat the line back to you after each one. Use the rhythm sticks to keep the beat as the class sings this version of "Little Nut Tree."

There Was an Old Woman

There was an old woman,

Who lived in a shoe.

She had so many children,

She didn't know what to do.

She gave them all broth

Without any bread.

Then kissed them all soundly

And put them to bed.

There Was an Old Woman (cont.)

Art Lesson

Skills

- develops an understanding of simple rubbing processes
- identifies texture
- creates a simple texture by rubbing
- recognizes shapes in the environment

Materials

- 8½" x 11" (22 cm x 28 cm) white construction paper, two per student
- copy of "There Was an Old Woman" (page 86)
- variety of crayons without wrappers
- butcher paper or chart paper
- student shoes (athletic)
- scissors, one per student
- pencils, one per student
- tape

Before the Lesson

1. Copy and enlarge the nursery rhyme "There Was an Old Woman" onto chart paper so that the class can see the words easily.

2. Remind students to try to wear shoes with interesting markings on the bottoms.

Procedure

1. Read the nursery rhyme "There Was an Old Woman" to the class, using the large display version. Read the rhyme again, tracking the words and allowing the class to join in if they are familiar with the rhyme.

2. Ask the students to sit in a circle with their feet pointing toward the middle. Ask if they notice any designs or shapes on the shoes that they see in the circle. Discuss their answers.

3. Ask the students to look at the undersides of the shoes. Ask, What types of shapes or patterns do you see now? Discuss the answers. A *shape* is a two-dimensional area with an edge that you can see. You can make a shape by drawing or painting lines on a paper. The edge of the shape creates a line.

4. Ask the students to each take off one of their shoes.

There Was an Old Woman *(cont.)*

Art Lesson *(cont.)*

Procedure *(cont.)*

5. Explain to the students that they will practice copying shapes and patterns by drawing what they see on the underside of their shoe.

6. Model for the students how to place the shoe in the center of a white piece of construction paper. Show them how to trace around the shoe with a pencil. Continue by showing them the pattern on the underside of the shoe that you are copying onto the shoe outline that you traced.

7. Show the students the finished example by holding up the shoe so that they can compare the underside of it to the shoe drawing.

8. Explain to the students that they are going to accent these shapes and designs by coloring them with crayon (or marker). Demonstrate a portion of this process. When finished with the entire shoe, use scissors to cut the shape out. Tape this shoe to the wall so that the students may have a sample of the process to follow.

9. Continue to model for the students as you explain that when they have finished, they will need to put the shoe back on and take the other one off. Ask, What do you notice about the patterns and designs on this shoe? Hopefully they will notice that they are the same.

10. Say, Feel the bottom of the shoe with your hand. Do you feel the shapes that you have drawn? What you are feeling is the quality of the surface of your shoe which is also known as *texture*. We will use a printmaking technique called *rubbing* to create this pattern on paper without actually having to draw it.

11. Using the other shoe, place a sheet of white paper over the underside of the shoe and use the flat side of a peeled crayon to create a rubbing. Rub the crayon back and forth across the paper (on the shoe) until the pattern of the shoe is recreated. Make sure that all parts of the underside of the shoe are rubbed, including the edges. Use scissors to cut out this shoe pattern. Tape this shoe pattern beside the first pattern. Ask, What are some similarities that you see between these two shoe patterns? What are some of the differences that you see?

12. Tape the shoe pairs to the wall as students finish so that it will appear that there are footprints climbing up the walls.

There Was an Old Woman (cont.)

O,   old,   old   wo‑man in a shoe,

had   so   man ‑ y kids,   what's she gon ‑ na do?

Music Lesson

Skills

- replicates simple music patterns
- knows the hand sign for the letter "o"
- recognizes the sound /o/

Materials

- medium rubber bands, two per student
- copy of nursery rhyme (page 86)
- pair of tap shoes (if available)
- chart paper or butcher paper
- juice can lids approximately 3" (8 cm) diameter
- copy of letter "o" jingle (above)
- parent letter (page 90), one per student

Before the Lesson

1. Enlarge and copy the letter "o" jingle onto butcher paper or chart paper.
2. Send home the completed parent letter before the lesson, allowing time to collect juice can lids.
3. Enlarge and copy "There Was an Old Woman" (page 86) onto butcher paper or chart paper.

Procedure

1. Read the nursery rhyme "There Was an Old Woman" aloud to the students, using the enlarged version of the rhyme. Read the rhyme a second time, tracking the words as you read them, allowing students to join in if they feel comfortable doing so.
2. Hold up the pair of tap shoes and ask, What type of shoes can make music? (*tap shoes*) Explain to the students that they will make tap shoes with juice can lids.
3. Read the letter "o" jingle aloud to the class, tracking the words on the chart.
4. Read the rhyme a second time, clapping the beat as you say the words. *Remind the students that for every beat that is clapped, there is a note on the staff.* Encourage students to recite the rhyme with you, clapping the beat as you point to the notes on the staff. Try the beat again, this time stomping the beat with your feet. Explain to the students that this is the beat that they will keep when they make their tap shoes.

There Was an Old Woman (cont.)

Music Lesson (cont.)

5. Give each student two rubber bands and two juice can lids. Model for the students how to hold the juice can lid under a shoe while wrapping the rubber band around the shoe. Repeat this procedure for the other shoe. Allow students time to put on their "taps." Help apply rubber bands.

6. Model how to keep the beat with your feet as you recite the rhyme. Reread the rhyme, letting students keep the beat with their feet.

7. Show the students the hand sign for the letter "o." (See example.) Explain that this is the sign that is used to represent the letter "o" for those who cannot hear or speak. This will also help them to remember the sound of the letter "o" as in the word *old* when they make this sign during the jingle. Sing the jingle again, using the hand sign for "o" when "o" is read on the chart.

Dear Parent(s),

On _____ we will be participating in a project using the nursery rhyme "There Was an Old Woman."

Please send two frozen juice can lids to school on or before this date. Please make sure that these metal lids are clean and do not have sharp edges.

Thank you!

_____
Teacher

Little Bo-Peep

Little Bo-Peep has lost her sheep,

And doesn't know where to find them;

Leave them alone,

And they'll come home,

Wagging their tails behind them.

Little Bo-Peep *(cont.)*

Art Lesson

Skills

- recognizes positive shapes
- uses scissors effectively
- recognizes negative shapes
- uses glue effectively

Materials

- Sheep Pattern (page 93), one per student
- 12" x 18" (30 cm x 46 cm) black construction paper, one per student
- 9" x 12" (23 cm x 30 cm) white construction paper, one per student
- black crayons, one per student
- scissors
- glue

Before the Lesson

1. Copy the sheep pattern on page 93 for each student.
2. Copy and enlarge the nursery rhyme "Little Bo-Peep" from page 91 onto butcher paper or chart paper. Display it in the classroom.

Procedure

1. Read the nursery rhyme "Little Bo-Peep" to the class, using the enlarged version. Read the rhyme again, inviting the students to join in, tracking the words as you read them.
2. Give each student a copy of the sheep pattern. Model steps 3–6 for the students as you cut out the sheep pattern. Then allow students to create their own images.
3. Trace the sheep that you cut out onto the center of the white construction paper.
4. Color the sheep with a black crayon as dark as possible.
5. Attach the white paper with the black sheep on it to the right side of the black construction paper. This will give the illusion that the black paper and the white paper are the same size.
6. Glue the white sheep pattern onto the center of the remaining black paper.
7. You should have a black sheep on white paper and a white sheep on black paper. Ask, Which one is a *negative* shape? Which one is a *positive* shape? When you create a pattern inside a shape that you've drawn, it makes it a positive shape. If you color in the space outside the object, leaving the inside uncolored, it creates a negative shape.

Little Bo-Peep *(cont.)*

Sheep Pattern

Little Bo-Peep (cont.)

P,   peep   at Lit - tle   Bo - Peep.   If

she's   not   care - ful she'll   lose   her   sheep!

Music Lesson

Skills

- recognizes the sound /p/
- knows the hand sign for the letter "p"
- rhymes

Materials

- butcher paper or chart paper

Before the Lesson

1. Copy and enlarge the jingle for the letter "p" onto butcher paper or chart paper.
2. Copy and enlarge the nursery rhyme "Little Bo-Peep" from page 91 onto butcher paper or chart paper.

Procedure

1. Read the nursery rhyme "Little Bo-Peep" to the class. Read the jingle a second time, inviting the students to join in as you track the words on the chart.

2. Show students the chart of the jingle for the letter "p." Read the rhyme to the class. Explain to the students that this jingle is similar to the nursery rhyme "Little Bo-Peep" but that this one will help them to remember the sound that the letter "p" makes as in *peep*. Say the jingle together, tracking the words on the chart as they are read.

3. Show the students the hand sign for the letter "p." (See example.) Explain that this is the sign that is used to represent the letter "p" for those who cannot hear or speak. This will also help them to remember "p" as they make this sign during the jingle. Repeat the jingle, using the hand sign for "p" when "p" is read on the chart.

Little Bo-Peep (cont.)

Music Lesson (cont.)

Procedure (cont.)

4. Explain that Little Bo-Peep rhymes with an animal name. Ask, What animal does Bo-Peep rhyme with? (*sheep*). What animal could be substituted when Little Bo-Peep is changed to Little Bo-Bow? (*cow*) Sing the jingle with other letter changes. To start, try these "b" substitutions:

Little Bo-Borse has lost her *horse*,
And doesn't know where to find it;
Leave it alone,
and it'll come home,
Wagging its tail behind it.

Little Bo-Big has lost her *pig*,
And doesn't know where to find it;
Leave it alone,
and it'll come home,
Wagging its tail behind it.

Little Bo-Buck has lost her *duck*,
And doesn't know where to find it;
Leave it alone,
and it'll come home,
Wagging its tail behind it.

Little Bo-Bicken has lost her *chicken*,
And doesn't know where to find it;
Leave it alone,
and it'll come home,
Wagging its tail behind it.

Little Bo-Bonkey has lost her donkey,
And doesn't know where to find it;
Leave it alone,
and it'll come home,
Wagging its tail behind it.

Jack Be Nimble

Jack be nimble,

Jack be quick,

Jack jump over

The candlestick.

Jack Be Nimble (cont.)

Art Lesson

Skills

- manipulates three dimensional shapes
- understands that shape is a form which can be either two- or three-dimensional

Materials

- old crayons—red, blue, yellow, green, orange, purple
- small paper cups, one per student
- birthday candles, one per student
- six large resealable baggies
- butcher paper or chart paper
- hot plate
- six pie pans
- scented oil
- candlestick
- six hammers

Before the Lesson

1. Copy and enlarge the nursery rhyme "Jack Be Nimble" (page 96) onto chart paper and display it in the classroom.
2. Arrange for adult assistance with hammering.

Procedure

1. Read the nursery rhyme "Jack Be Nimble" to the class using the large version. Track the words as you read them.
2. Show the students a candlestick. Ask, What do you think candles are made out of? Take answers. Explain that candles are made of wax. Ask, Do you know of any other things that are made of wax? Did you know that crayons are also made of wax? Students will make Jack's candlestick using wax crayons.
3. Divide students into small groups and give them a pile of crayons to sort by color. Make a pile of red, a pile of blue, a pile of green, etc. until all crayons are grouped. When students have finished, put all the reds together in one large group, continuing until all of the colors are separated into color groups.
4. While students are still in small groups, redistribute the crayons, keeping them in color groups. Take the wrappers off of all crayons and break them in half as many times as possible.
5. Put each pile of crayons in a separate, gallon-sized, resealable bag. Make sure that all of the air is released from the bag.

Jack Be Nimble (cont.)

Art Lesson (cont.)

Procedure (cont.)

6. Model for the students as you tap on the bag with the hammer, breaking the crayons inside the bag. Explain that they will take turns doing this, but it must be done carefully and everyone's hands and feet should be away from the tapping area.

7. After the crayons are crushed, collect the baggies. Place a pie pan on the hot plate and empty the bag of red crayons into the pie tin. Do not turn on the hot plate yet.

8. Give each student a birthday candle and a small paper cup. Explain that they will use this small candle in order to have a wick to burn in their crayon candle. Discuss with the students the process that they have participated in so far. Ask, How has the shape of our crayons changed? Review that first the crayon was whole, then it was broken into smaller bits, and then crushed into tiny bits. Ask, How will the crayon change when we melt it? How will the shape change when we pour it into the paper cup?

9. Turn on the hot plate, stirring the melted crayons until smooth. Collect cups from all of the students who would like to have a red candle. Add several drops of scented oil to the mixture in the pie pan.

   Teacher Note: Students should not participate in pouring the hot wax into the cup. Another adult should place the birthday candle in place at the center of the cup vertically until the crayon wax begins to harden. Set the candles in an isolated place until they are cool and have hardened completely.

10. Repeat the melting process with each of the other bags of crayons, changing pie pans each time, until all colors have been turned into candles. Ask, How did the shape of the crayons change? Direct students in a discussion that will help them understand the changes that the crayons went through to become candles.

11. After the candles have hardened and cooled, tear the cup off of the candles. The candle will hold the shape of the cup. Remind students that they should always let an adult light their candles, and they should keep a plate or other flame-resistant object underneath it while it is burning. Never leave a candle unattended and never play with fire.

12. Role play the nursery rhyme, using the homemade candlesticks.

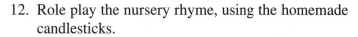

Jack Be Nimble (cont.)

Music Lesson

Skills
- recognizes the sound /q/
- knows the hand sign for the letter "q"
- differentiates between fast (quick) and slow

Materials
- candlestick
- butcher paper or chart paper

Before the Lesson
1. Copy and enlarge the jingle for the letter "q" onto butcher paper or chart paper.
2. Copy and enlarge the nursery rhyme "Jack Be Nimble" (page 96) onto butcher paper or chart paper.

Procedure
1. Read the nursery rhyme "Jack Be Nimble" to the class. Read the jingle a second time, inviting the students to join in as you track the words on the chart.

2. Show students the chart of the jingle for the letter "q." Read the jingle to the class. Explain to the students that this jingle is similar to the nursery rhyme "Jack Be Nimble" but that this one will help them to remember the sound that the letter "q" makes as in *quick*. Say the jingle together, tracking the words on the chart as they are read.

3. Show the students the hand sign for the letter "q." (See example.) Explain that this is the sign that is used to represent the letter "q" for those who cannot hear or speak. This will also help them to remember "q" as they make this sign during the jingle. Repeat the jingle, using the hand sign for "q" when "q" is read on the chart.

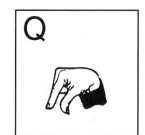

Jack Be Nimble *(cont.)*

Music Lesson *(cont.)*

4. Sing the jingle slowly. Sing the jingle quickly. Ask the students if they recognize the difference between the two ways that you sang the jingle. (One version was slow, the other was fast.)

5. Explain that students are going to play a game that is called Johnny Be Quick.

Directions for Johnny Be Quick Game

1. Have the students sit in a large circle. Make sure there is room to run around the circle. Hand a candle to one student. He or she will be "Johnny."

2. "Johnny" skips around the outside of the circle of children as all sing the jingle for the letter "q."

3. "Johnny" will lay the candle behind another child, who chases him or her around the circle, trying to tag him or her. "Johnny" tries to reach the empty space in the circle (where the other child had been stitting) without being tagged.

4. If successful, "Johnny" is "safe." If not, he or she must sit in the center of the circle. The game continues with the other child as "Johnny."

Jack and Jill

Jack and Jill

Went up the hill

To fetch a pail of water.

Jack fell down,

And broke his crown,

And Jill came tumbling after.

Then up Jack got

And home did trot

As fast as he could caper;

And went to bed to mend his head

With vinegar and brown paper.

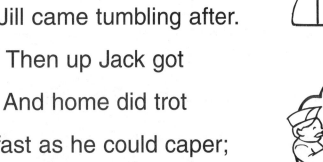
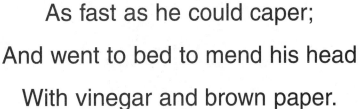

Jack and Jill *(cont.)*

Art Lesson

Skills

- identifies rough, smooth, soft, and bumpy textures
- creates a simple texture

Materials

- 12" x 18" (30 cm x 46 cm) newsprint, one per student
- sample pieces of cotton, sandpaper, and paper
- black permanent markers, one per student
- pencils, one per student
- chart paper or butcher paper
- copies of pages 104–106
- fabric scraps
- hair brush
- crayons
- mirrors
- yarn

Before the Lesson

1. Copy and enlarge the nursery rhyme "Jack and Jill" (page 101) onto butcher paper or chart paper.
2. Copy pages 104 and 105 onto cardstock paper or trace the figures onto poster board. Each student will need either a Jack or a Jill pattern.
3. Copy page 106 onto cardstock paper or trace clothing patterns onto poster board for students to share.

Procedure

1. Read the nursery rhyme "Jack and Jill," using the enlarged version on chart paper. Track the words as you read them the second time so students may join in if they already know the words.
2. Discuss the nursery rhyme "Jack and Jill." Ask, What do we have in common with Jack and Jill? Write answers on chart paper as students come up with ideas. One of the ideas that students may or may not come up with is that Jack and Jill were children, just like they are. Ask, What are some clues in the rhyme that make us think that they were children? Write down ideas that the students may have on chart paper.
3. As students come up with ideas, begin to direct them towards what they will need to think about in the art lesson, which are human features. While writing student ideas on chart paper, begin drawing a human childlike figure, which will guide students' thoughts toward human features. (*hair, eyes, mouth*) Add these features as students come up with them. As students become more distinct about what they see, explain that they are seeing the details that they will need to pay attention to when drawing a portrait.
4. Explain that today, students are going to learn how to draw a human portrait. A *portrait* is a picture of a person. It can be drawn, painted, or photographed.

Jack and Jill (cont.)

Art Lesson (cont.)

Procedure (cont.)

5. Have students look in the mirror. Have them look at the features of their faces. Point out that each child's features may be different from others in the class. Ask, How long is your hair? What color are your eyes? What shape is your nose? What shape is your mouth?

6. Give each student a piece of paper and a pencil to attempt a self-portrait drawing. If possible, allow the students to look in a mirror while drawing. If mirrors are unavailable, allow students to divide into partners and draw each other. Remind each student to think about the shape of his or her face and then to add details.

Paper Dolls

1. Allow students to feel the cotton ball, the hair brush, the sandpaper, and the paper sample. Ask the following questions and list the answers.

   • What are some words that describe the way the cotton ball feels? Can you think of other things that feel like cotton balls?

   • What are some words that describe the way the hair brush feels? What are some other things that feel like the bristles on a hair brush?

   • What are some words that describe the way the sandpaper feels? Can you think of other things that feel like sandpaper?

   • What are some words that describe the way the paper feels? What are other things that feel like paper?

2. Explain that the words they have just used to describe the way that these objects feel also describe their *texture*. Mention that texture often makes works of art more interesting.

3. Discuss the textures that will be used in this project. Each student may choose to make a "Jack" doll or a "Jill" doll. It will be used later to role-play the nursery rhyme "Jack and Jill."

4. Give each student a copy of page 104 or 105 (Jack or Jill), preferably copied on cardstock paper or traced onto poster board paper for durability.

5. Model for the students how to cut out the shape. Explain that they may choose clothes from page 106 to trace and cut out of fabric. Paste the fabric to the doll. Use portrait-making techniques to complete the doll's face. Glue yarn to the head for hair.

6. When finished, create a setting for the rhyme such as a rug with something underneath which will create the effect of a hill. Allow students to recreate the rhyme using their paper dolls.

Jack and Jill (cont.)

Art Lesson (cont.)

Jill Pattern

Jack and Jill *(cont.)*

Jack Pattern

Jack and Jill *(cont.)*

Art Lesson *(cont.)*

Clothing Patterns

Jack and Jill *(cont.)*

R,   run, run up the hill but

don't fall down with Jack and Jill!

Music Lesson

Skills

- recognizes the sound /r/
- knows the hand sign for the letter "r"
- identifies action words

Before the Lesson

1. Copy and enlarge the jingle for the letter "r" onto butcher paper or chart paper.

2. Copy and enlarge the nursery rhyme "Jack and Jill" from page 101 onto butcher paper or chart paper.

Procedure

1. Read the nursery rhyme "Jack and Jill" to the class. Read the rhyme a second time, inviting the students to join in as you track the words on the chart.

2. Show students the chart of the jingle for the letter "r." Read the jingle to the class. Explain to the students that this jingle is similar to the nursery rhyme "Jack and Jill" but that this one will help us to remember the sound that the letter "r" makes as in *run*. Say the jingle together, tracking the words on the chart as they are read.

3. Show the students the hand sign for the letter "r." (See example.) Explain that this is the sign that is used to represent the letter "r" for those who cannot hear or speak. This will also help them to remember "r" as they make this sign during the jingle. Repeat the jingle, using the hand sign for "r" when "r" is read on the chart.

4. Explain to the students that Jack and Jill were running. *Run* is an action word. Run tells us how Jack and Jill were moving. Ask the students to brainstorm other ways that Jack and Jill could have reached the top of the hill—skip, walk, bounce, crawl, gallop, jump, roll, tip-toe. Have students sing and act out the new jingle, substituting action words in the place of *run*.

Simple Simon

Simple Simon met a pieman,
Going to the fair.
Says Simple Simon to the pieman,
Let me taste your ware.
Says the pieman to Simple Simon,
Show me first your penny.
Says Simple Simon to the pieman,
Indeed I have not any.

Simple Simon went a-fishing
For to catch a whale;
All the water he had got
Was in his mother's pail.
Simple Simon went to look
If plums grew on a thistle;
He pricked his finger very much
Which made poor Simon whistle.

Simple Simon (cont.)

Art Lesson

Skills

- manipulates and experiments with paint
- uses scissors effectively
- uses a pattern effectively

Materials

- whale pattern (page 110)
- heavy paper for each student
- pie pan, one per group of students
- black and white tempera paint
- crayons or markers
- paintbrushes
- poster board
- white paper
- scissors
- pencils
- water
- tape

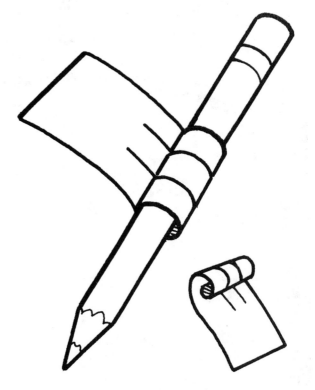

Before the Lesson

1. Copy the whale pattern onto poster board as many times as needed for student patterns. Cut the patterns out.
2. Copy the spout pattern onto white paper. Make one for each student.
3. Copy and enlarge the nursery rhyme "Simple Simon" onto chart paper or butcher paper and display it in the classroom.

Procedure

1. Read the nursery rhyme "Simple Simon" to the class using the enlarged version. Reread the nursery rhyme, encouraging students to read the rhyme with you, tracking the words.
2. Ask, What did Simple Simon go fishing for in this rhyme? (*a whale*) Explain that they will be making Simple Simon's whale through a technique called *tempera wash*.
3. Model for the students as you trace the whale pattern onto heavy paper. Have students trace and cut out their own whales.
4. Pour a dab of black tempera paint and a dab of white tempera paint into each pie pan and add water until the consistency is about half paint and half water.
5. Using paintbrushes stir the mixture. Paint the whales with paintbrushes. Fill in the entire shape. Allow the paint to dry.
6. Add an eye and a mouth to each whale, using a crayon, construction paper, or markers.
7. Cut out the spout pattern piece. Carefully cut on the three dashed lines. Curl the strips as shown above. Tape the spout to the back of the whale.

Simple Simon *(cont.)*

Art Lesson *(cont.)*

Whale Pattern

Spout

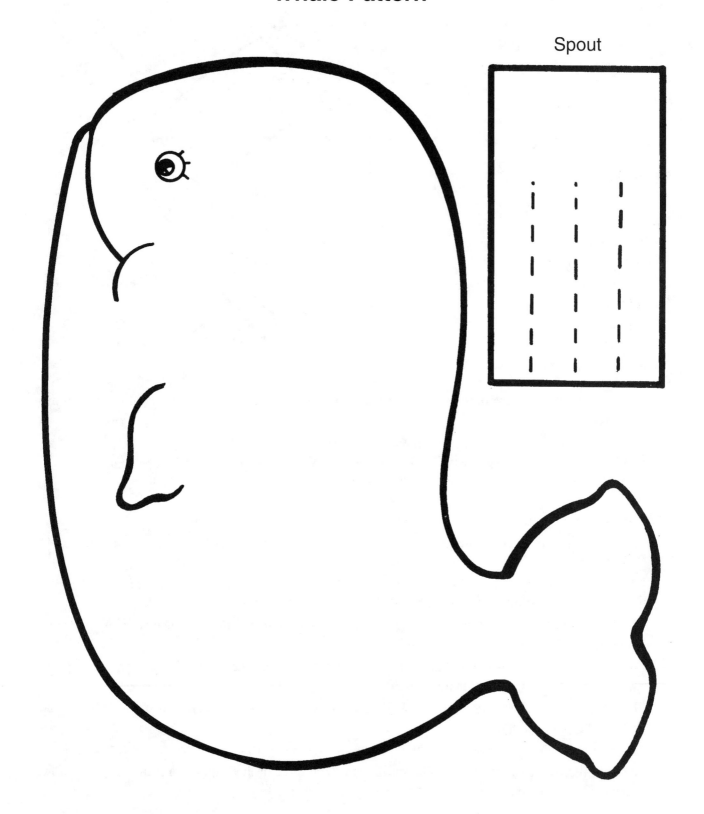

Simple Simon (cont.)

S,   Si - mon,   Sim - ple   Si - mon,

we   all   know   he   met   a   pie - man!

Music Lesson

Skills

- keeps a steady beat
- recognizes the sound /s/
- creates musical instruments
- knows the hand sign for the letter "s"

Materials

- small pie tins, two per student
- 12" (30 cm) streamers in assorted colors, three per student
- pennies, three per student
- hot glue/hot glue gun
- butcher paper or chart paper

Teacher Note: Teachers and other adults should always be at hand to apply hot glue. Students should not use the hot glue guns themselves.

Before the Lesson

1. Copy and enlarge the nursery rhyme "Simple Simon" (page 108) onto butcher paper or chart paper and display in the classroom.
2. Copy and enlarge the jingle for the letter "s" onto butcher paper or chart paper.

Procedure

1. Read the nursery rhyme "Simple Simon," using the enlarged version. Reread the rhyme, tracking the words and inviting students to join in saying the words with you.
2. Since Simple Simon met a pieman, we will make music with pie tins. Model the activity for the students as you explain. Hand each student two pie pans. Lay three pennies inside one pie pan.
3. Apply glue around the lip of the pie pan with the pennies lying inside.

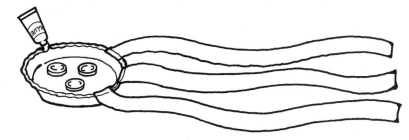

Simple Simon *(cont.)*

Music Lesson *(cont.)*

Procedure *(cont.)*

4. Choose three colors of streamers and lay the top of each one side-by-side on the glue along the lip of the pie pan.

5. Press the other pie pan upside down so that the lips of each pie pan press together. Allow the project time to dry.

6. Read the letter "s" jingle for Simple Simon from the chart. Explain to the students that this jingle is similar to the nursery rhyme "Simple Simon" but that this one will help them remember the sound that the letter "s" makes as in *Simple* and *Simon*. Say the jingle together, tracking the words on the chart as they are read.

7. Show the students the hand sign for the letter "s." (See example.) Explain that this is the sign that is used to represent the letter "s" for those who cannot hear or speak. This will also help them to remember "s" as they make this sign during the jingle. Sing the jingle again, using the hand sign for "s" when "s" is read on the chart.

8. There are four beats to each line in this little song. Demonstrate the beat with your pie-pan shaker. Explain to the students that even though the words may speed up or slow down, the beat remains the same. Invite the students to join you the second time.

9. Divide the class in half. Explain to them that while keeping a steady beat with the pie-pan shakers, they will do a round. That means that one group will start the rhyme and when they begin the second line, the other group will begin with the first line. Keep repeating the rhyme until each group has said the entire rhyme four times.

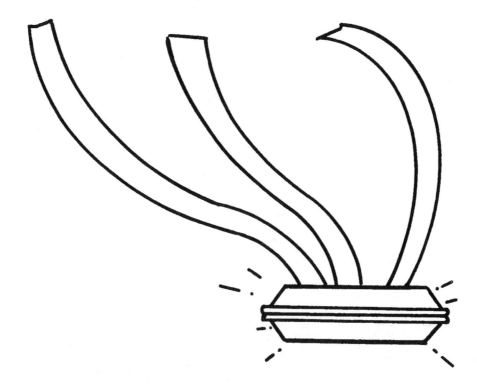

Polly Put the Kettle On

Polly put the kettle on,

Polly put the kettle on,

Polly put the kettle on,

We'll all have tea.

Sukey take it off again,

Sukey take it off again,

Sukey take it off again,

They've all gone away!

Polly Put the Kettle On (cont.)

Art Lesson

Skills

- understands that space is the area around shapes
- uses art media to explore patterns
- recognizes that some spaces are empty
- uses scissors effectively
- understands that a pattern is a repetition of designs
- understands that patterns exist in everyday objects

Materials

- samples of teacup and saucer sets with interesting design patterns
- copy of "Polly Put the Kettle On" (page 113)
- copy of the teacup and tea bag for each student (page 115)
- crayons or markers
- scissors
- string
- hole punch
- tape

Before the Lesson

1. Copy and enlarge the nursery rhyme "Polly Put the Kettle On" on butcher paper or chart paper.

2. Display the teacup and saucer sets. Allow students time to examine the patterns on each cup and saucer.

Procedure

1. Read the nursery rhyme "Polly Put the Kettle On" to the class, using the enlarged version. Read the rhyme again, tracking the words with your finger, and encouraging students to recite the poem along with you.

2. Show the students the different examples of teacups and saucers. Encourage students to look at the teacups and saucers. What is interesting about them? (*different designs, different shapes*) Have you seen other designs on teacups at other places? Discuss until the students understand that teacups and saucers come in many different designs and sizes. Point out that the artists who create the designs usually use a technique called patterning. *Patterning* is the process of repeating a design over and over. The design can be anything, but it must be repeated to create a successful cup design.

Polly Put the Kettle On (cont.)

Art Lesson (cont.)

Procedure (cont.)

3. Model for the students an example of patterning on an enlarged copy of a teacup.

4. Ask the students questions about the patterns modeled for them. Help them understand that the patterns can go around the cup from left to right or from top to bottom.

5. Model for the students an example of patterning with color. Revert to the real cup examples to explain color patterns as well as design patterns. Model steps 6–9 for students.

6. Cut out the cup. Design a pattern for the cup.

7. Cut out and color the tea bag.

8. Attach string to the tea bag by using the hole punch to make the hole and tie a string to it. Tape the string behind the cup, so that it gives the illusion of a tea bag in the cup.

Polly Put the Kettle On *(cont.)*

T,   tea,   let's all have tea!

Pol – ly put the ket – tle on for you   and   me!

Music Lesson

Skills

- differentiates between high and low pitch
- creates different levels of pitch
- recognizes the sound /t/
- knows the hand sign for the letter "t"

Materials

- 4 large teacups
- spoons
- pitcher of water
- enlarged copy of nursery rhyme (page 113)

Procedure

1. Read "Polly Put the Kettle On," using the enlarged version on chart paper. Reread the rhyme, inviting the students to read along with you, while tracking the words with your finger.

2. Explain that they are going to read it again, only this time they will read it using a high pitched voice. Read it together in a high voice. Read the rhyme again with the students using a low voice.

3. Discuss the difference in how the rhyme sounds when saying it in a high voice and a low voice. Discuss what causes voices to go up and down. Explain that when they study high and low sounds, they are studying *pitch*. It is fairly easy to control the pitch of our voices, but is it easy to control the pitch of objects? Introduce an experiment with pitch and Polly's teacups.

4. Put the four large teacups in a row on the floor or on a table where all students can see them clearly. Take the pitcher of water and put a very small amount of water in the first teacup. Add a little more water to the second teacup, a little more to the third, and fill the fourth teacup to the top with water. Ask, Will the pitch be higher or lower when I strike the first cup, filled with a small amount of water, than the pitch in the cup that is full of water? Take guesses.

5. Strike the first cup, containing a small amount of water, with a spoon as the students listen. Then, strike the fourth cup, which contains a lot of water, as the students listen. Ask, What did you hear?

6. Now play a game. Select one student to come to the front of the room. All the other students will stand with their eyes closed. When the student in the front of the room strikes the cup, decide if it is a high pitch or a low pitch. If the pitch is high, students will raise up their arms, if the pitch is low, students will squat down. Allow as many students as possible to come up to the front.

7. Show the students the hand sign for the letter "t." Sing the jingle again using the hand sign for the letter "t."

Little Boy Blue

Little Boy Blue come blow your horn.

The cow's in the meadow,

The sheep's in the corn.

But where is the little boy

Tending the sheep?

He's under the haystack fast asleep.

Will you wake him?

No, not I,

For if I do,

He's sure to cry.

Little Boy Blue (cont.)

Art Lesson

Skills

- creates texture
- uses line to create recognizable figures
- experiments with paint

Materials

- 12" x 18" (30 cm x 46 cm) white construction paper, one per student
- copy of "Little Boy Blue" (page 117)
- glue in squeeze bottles
- pencils or stir sticks
- blue food coloring
- watercolor paints, one box per two students
- paintbrushes, one per student
- water

Before the Lesson

1. Copy and enlarge the nursery rhyme "Little Boy Blue" on butcher paper or chart paper.

2. Mix blue food coloring into all but one squeeze bottle of glue.

Procedure

1. Read the nursery rhyme "Little Boy Blue" to the class, using the enlarged version. Read the rhyme again, encouraging the students to join in with you, while tracking the words.

2. Explain to the students that they are going to draw their own version of Little Boy Blue, creating texture using blue glue. Add a few drops of blue food coloring to the remaining bottle of white glue. Stir it as well as possible with a long, thin stir stick or a pencil. Replace the lid tightly. Students will enjoy seeing the process of making colored glue.

3. Model each step for the students as you draw a picture of your version of Little Boy Blue. First, draw very lightly with a pencil. Explain to the students that there will be as many versions of Little Boy Blue as there are students in the class.

4. Use the blue glue to trace over the picture that you drew, trying to keep a continuous flow of glue coming out of the bottle. This will help prevent big blobs of glue from coming out in one spot.

5. Lay the picture flat and let it dry over night.

6. Using a small paintbrush, dip the brush into water and then into the watercolor of your choice. Begin by filling in one of the enclosed glue shapes with one color. Change colors and fill in another shape. Continue until all the shapes are filled in. Allow the paint to dry.

7. When the project is completely dry, enjoy feeling the texture of the line that you have created. Little Boy Blue with blue glue is fun to do!

Little Boy Blue (cont.)

U, un – der, un – der the hay,

Li – tle Boy Blue was sleep-ing a – way.

Music Lesson

Skills

- recognizes the sound /u/
- recognizes brass instruments by sight
- knows the hand sign for the letter "u"
- recognizes brass instruments by sound

Materials

- various brass instruments or pictures of brass instruments (page 120)
- recordings of brass instruments

Before the Lesson

1. Copy and enlarge the jingle for the letter "u" onto butcher paper or chart paper.

2. Copy and enlarge the nursery rhyme "Little Boy Blue" from page 117 onto butcher paper or chart paper.

Procedure

1. Read the nursery rhyme "Little Boy Blue" to the class. Read the rhyme a second time, inviting the students to join in as you track the words on the chart.

2. Show students the chart of the jingle for the letter "u." Read the rhyme to the class. Explain to the students that this jingle is similar to the nursery rhyme "Little Boy Blue" but that this one will help them to remember the sound that the letter "u" makes as in *under*. Say the jingle together, tracking the words on the chart as they are read.

3. Show the students the hand sign for the letter "u." (See example.) Explain that this is the sign that is used to represent the letter "u" for those who cannot hear or speak. This will also help them to remember "u" as we make this sign during the jingle. Say the jingle again, using the hand sign for "u" when "u" is read on the chart.

4. Explain that Little Boy Blue had a horn. A horn is a brass instrument. There are several types of brass instruments. Share the pictures (page 120) and recordings of brass instruments with the class.

Little Boy Blue (cont.)

Music Lesson (cont.)

Brass Instruments

Trumpet

French Horn

Saxophone

Tuba

There Was
a Crooked Man

There was a crooked man,

And he went a crooked mile.

He found a crooked sixpence

Against a crooked stile.

He bought a crooked cat,

Which caught a crooked mouse.

And they all lived together

In a crooked little house.

There Was a Crooked Man (cont.)

Art Lesson

Skills

- manipulates and experiments with paper
- experiments with dimensionality

Materials

- Crooked Art Template (page 124), two per student
- white paper, two per student
- crayons or markers
- butcher paper or chart paper

Before the Lesson

1. Copy and enlarge the nursery rhyme "There Was a Crooked Man" (page 121) onto butcher paper or chart paper. Display it in the classroom.

2. Make two copies of the Crooked Art Template for each student. One copy will be given to each student at the beginning of the lesson. (Procedure 4)

3. Use the remaining copies of the Crooked Art Template to create a folded sheets of paper for each student. Cut out the template on the solid, outer line. Fold the paper back and forth (fan-like) creating six sections. The folds will be the same length and width as the strips of paper formed from the students' drawings. This folded copy of the Crooked Art Template will be given to the students after they have colored their pictures.

Procedure

1. Read the rhyme "There Was a Crooked Man" using the enlarged version. Read the rhyme again, tracking the words as they are read and encouraging students to recite the rhyme along with you.

2. Explain that since this rhyme is about things that are crooked, they are going to do some crooked art.

3. Give each student a copy of the Crooked Art Template from page 124. Point out that it has solid lines across it and a dashed line in the middle. Have students cut on the dashed line, creating two separate sheets of paper with lines on them forming three strips or sections.

4. Have students draw a picture that will fill the entire space on both sheets of lined paper.

   Teacher Note: Make sure that the picture is drawn so that the paper is wider than it is tall. If you want to stay thematic, have the students draw a large, crooked house on one of the pages and a man on the other pages.

5. Be sure to color the background so that the entire page is colored. When the drawings have been completed, have the students cut on the two solid lines on each page.

6. Now comes the tricky part. Have students lay the strips down in order using the numbers on the side of the pictures. Number one should be at the top and number six should be the last strip on the bottom.

7. Next, give the students the pre-folded Crooked Art Template. Have the students glue the strips onto the folded paper, matching the numbers of their strips to the template. Number one will be at the top of the page and number six will be at the bottom. When the strips have all been glued in place, students can re-crease the folds (fan-like) on their papers.

There Was a Crooked Man (cont.)

Art Lesson (cont.)

Procedure (cont.)

8. The crooked art that they have created should create an interesting study on dimensionality. Have students look down at the paper from the top, tilting it so that they can see only one of the pictures drawn. Tilting the paper the other way should enable students to see the other picture. Have students vary the amount of tilt when they hold the page and the amount of fold to the paper.

9. For additional views, lay the folded paper on a table and walk around the table, viewing it from different angles. Try walking near the table and farther away.

There Was a Crooked Man (cont.)

Art Lesson *(cont.)*

Crooked Art Template

	1
	2
	3
	4
	5
	6

There Was a Crooked Man (cont.)

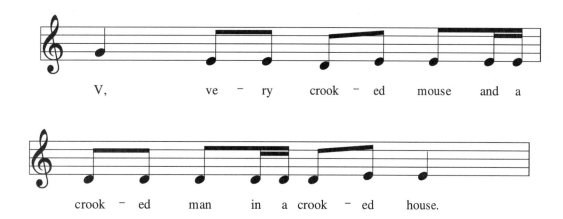

V, ve – ry crook – ed mouse and a

crook – ed man in a crook – ed house.

Music Lesson

Skills
- recognizes the /v/ sound
- knows the hand sign for the letter "v"
- differentiates between high and low notes

Before the Lesson
- Copy and enlarge the jingle for the letter "v" on this page onto butcher paper or chart paper.
- Copy and enlarge the nursery rhyme "There Was a Crooked Man" from page 121 onto butcher paper or chart paper.

Procedure

1. Read the nursery rhyme "There Was a Crooked Man" to the class. Read the rhyme a second time, inviting the students to join in as you track the words on the chart.

2. Show students the chart of the jingle for the letter "v." Read the jingle to the class. Explain to the students that this jingle is similar to the nursery rhyme "There Was a Crooked Man" but that this one will help them to remember the sound that the letter "v" makes as in *very*. Say the jingle together, tracking the words on the chart as they are read.

3. Show the students the hand sign for the letter "v." (See example.) Explain that this is the sign that is used to represent the letter "v" for those who cannot hear or speak. This will also help them to remember "v" as they make this sign during the jingle. Repeat the jingle, using the hand sign for "v" when "v" is read on the chart.

4. Explain that when singing, it is important to try to match notes in music. Play a note on the piano (keyboard, xylophone, guitar, etc.). Try to hum on the same note as the note played on the piano. Practice this with a variety of high notes and low notes. Point out that some notes were high and some notes were low. Are they easy to differentiate? Make the "v" hand sign. Explain that there will be a variety of notes played. Make the "v" sign very high in the air if the note is high (like the very crooked house) and make the "v" sign very low to the ground if the note is low (like a very crooked mouse). Practice this exercise as many times as desired.

Humpty Dumpty

Humpty Dumpty

Sat on a wall.

Humpty Dumpty

Had a great fall.

All the king's horses

And all the king's men

Couldn't put Humpty

together again.

Humpty Dumpty *(cont.)*

Art Lesson

Skills

- uses papier-mâché to construct simple forms
- uses papier-mâché to create original and expressive objects
- designs the surface of a three-dimensional, papier-mâché object
- recognizes papier-mâché objects as being sculptural
- reinforces understanding of art and the creation of art through successful experiences in papier-mâché construction

Materials

- Humpty Dumpty patterns, page 130
- large balloons, one per student
- white and black tempera paint
- parent letter, (page 129) one per student
- hot glue and glue gun
- glue
- bowls
- funnel
- yarn for hair (optional)
- newspapers (may be precut into strips)
- paintbrushes, one per student
- old socks, one pair per student
- black and white felt
- pencils
- water
- beans, one cup per student
- tape
- liquid starch

Teacher Note: Teachers and other adults should always be at hand to apply hot glue. Students should not use the hot glue guns themselves.

Before the Lesson

1. Send the parent letter (page 129) home a few days before the project is to begin.
2. Copy and enlarge the rhyme "Humpty Dumpty" (page 126) onto chart paper or butcher paper so that the students can view it during the lesson.
3. Prepare the starch mixture. Blend one cup (240 mL) of water, one cup (240 mL) of starch, and about 2 cups (480 mL) of glue in a large bowl for each student. Mix it with a spoon until blended.
4. Precut the strips of newspaper, if necessary.

Procedure

1. Read the rhyme "Humpty Dumpty" to the class. Track the words as you read them. Read the rhyme again, allowing the students to join in.
2. Discuss the rhyme. Mention that the rhyme never says that Humpty Dumpty is actually an egg. We think that he is an egg because historically the nursery rhyme depicts an egg in the illustrations. We also know that Humpty Dumpty couldn't be put back together again, and eggs are hard to put back together again once they break.

Humpty Dumpty (cont.)

Art Lesson (cont.)

Procedure (cont.)

3. Explain that each student is going to make a
Humpty Dumpty, but that the Humpty Dumptys
made in class will not be as breakable as a real
egg since they will be made of papier-mâché.
Papier-mâché is an art medium which is formed
through a combination of paper and paste, that
when put together, forms objects. It is a
sculptural process, which means that the end
product will be a three-dimensional figure.
Humpty Dumpty's body is actually a balloon
(form) covered with newspapers, glue, and
starch (papier-mâché) which will hold it
together.

Making Humpty Dumpty

1. Blow up a large balloon and knot the end.
(Students may need help with this step.)

2. Place the balloon inside a bowl so that it will not
roll around on the table while the newspaper
strips are applied.

3. Dip a strip of newspaper into the starch mixture
and lay it on the balloon. Continue this process
until the entire balloon is covered with
newspaper strips. Smooth the surface with a
paintbrush as the strips are applied to avoid
lumps. The newspaper pieces must lie as flat as
possible. When the top half of the balloon is
completely covered with papier-mâché, turn the
balloon upside down so that the part of the
balloon that was lying in the bowl is facing up.
Continue covering the remaining part of the
balloon with the newspaper strips that have been
dipped into the mixture.

4. Let the papier-mâché balloon dry for one day.

5. Choose an area to be the back of Humpty
Dumpty. Poke a hole with a pencil into the
backside to pop the balloon. Funnel one cup of
beans into the hole and tape over the hole. This
will help Humpty Dumpty to sit without rolling.

6. Paint the entire balloon with white tempera paint.

128

Humpty Dumpty *(cont.)*

Art Lesson *(cont.)*

Making Humpty Dumpty *(cont.)*

7. Paint eyes and a mouth on Humpty Dumpty using black paint.

8. Use a pair of old socks for Humpty Dumpty's legs. Allow a teacher to use a hot glue gun to attach the legs to the bottom of the papier mâché egg.

9. Use the Humpty Dumpty pattern and the felt (black or white) for the arms. Allow a teacher to use a hot glue gun to attach the arms, shoes and hat.

10. Yarn hair may also be added if you wish. Humpty Dumpty will look so cute sitting on your very own wall in your room!

Dear Parent(s),

On _____ we will be working with the nursery rhyme "Humpty Dumpty." We will be making our own Humpty Dumpty out of papier-mâché. We will need donations of newspaper and one (1) pair of old socks per student. These will be used as Humpty Dumpty's legs. Please send these items as soon as you can.

Thank you!

_____
Teacher

Humpty Dumpty *(cont.)*

Patterns

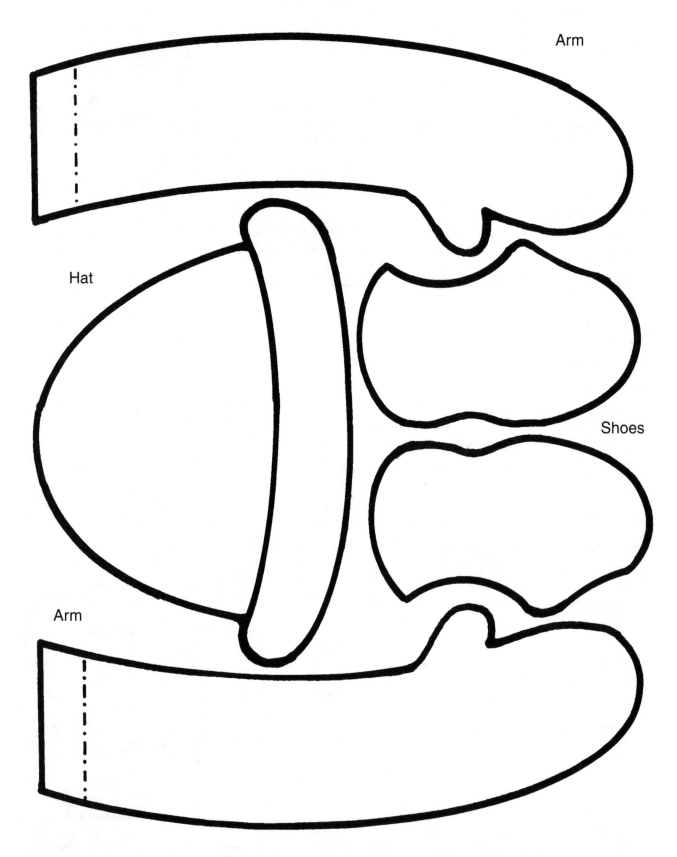

Arm

Hat

Arm

Shoes

Humpty Dumpty (cont.)

W,   wall,   off   the   wall.

Hump – ty   Dump – ty   had a great   fall!

Music Lesson

Skills

- recognizes the sound /w/
- predicts object sounds
- knows the hand sign for the letter "w"

Materials

- plastic eggs filled with shakable objects (pennies, rocks, sand, rice, marbles, or water)
- butcher paper or chart paper

Before the Lesson

1. Copy and enlarge the jingle for the letter "w" onto butcher paper or chart paper.
2. Copy and enlarge the nursery rhyme "Humpty Dumpty" (page 126) onto butcher paper or chart paper.
3. Fill the plastic eggs with a variety of different-sounding items.

Procedure

1. Read the nursery rhyme "Humpty Dumpty" to the class. Read the rhyme a second time, inviting the students to join in as you track the words on the chart.
2. Show students the chart of the jingle for the letter "w." Read the rhyme to the class. Explain to the students that this jingle is similar to the "Humpty Dumpty" nursery rhyme but that this one will help them to remember the sound that the letter "w" makes in the word *wall*. Say the jingle together, tracking the words on the chart as they are read.

Humpty Dumpty (cont.)

Music Lesson (cont.)

Procedure (cont.)

3. Show the students the hand sign for the letter "w." Explain that this is the sign that is used to represent the letter "w" for those who cannot hear or speak. This will also help them to remember "w" as they make this sign during the jingle. Say the jingle again, using the hand sign for "w" when "w" is read on the chart.

4. Explain that Humpty Dumpty was thought to have been an egg. Show students the plastic eggs with hidden objects inside them. Pass the first egg around so that each student may shake it and predict what object may be inside. When each student has had a chance to handle the egg, take guesses as to what might be inside. Continue this procedure with the other eggs.

5. Open each egg and reveal the objects inside to the students. Explain that objects such as these may be used as instruments. Each one makes a unique sound.

6. Give each student an empty, plastic egg. Have each student find an object that will fit inside the egg that will make its own unique sound. Allow the students to play their new instruments while singing the jingle for the letter "w."

Baa, Baa, Black Sheep

Baa, baa, black sheep,

Have you any wool?

Yes sir, yes sir,

Three bags full;

One for my master,

And one for the dame,

And one for the little boy

Who lives down the lane.

Baa, Baa, Black Sheep *(cont.)*

Art Lesson

Skills

- paints with texture
- accomplishes, as a member of a cooperative group, a type of mural that could not be accomplished individually
- understands the mural process and participates in its creation

Materials

- "How to Draw a Lamb" work sheet, (page 70)
- black and green tempera paint
- cotton balls
- paint trays
- butcher paper
- crayons

Before the Lesson

1. Copy and enlarge the nursery rhyme "Baa, Baa, Black Sheep" onto butcher paper or chart paper and display in the classroom.

2. Put long strips of white butcher paper over tables or onto the floor. Arrange one large strip for each group.

3. Put black tempera paint into pie pans or paint trays for each cooperative group.

4. Put green tempera paint into pie pans or paint trays for each cooperative group.

5. Put a large container of crayons at each cooperative work area.

6. Copy and enlarge the "How to Draw Lamb" page onto butcher paper or chart paper.

Procedure

1. Read the nursery rhyme "Baa, Baa, Black Sheep" to the class using the enlarged version. Reread the nursery rhyme, inviting the students to read it along with you, tracking the words as they are read.

2. Discuss the nursery rhyme. Remind students that a baby sheep is called a lamb. Ask, Has anyone here ever touched a sheep or a lamb before? What do they feel like? Explain that when they talk about the way something feels we are talking about its texture. *Texture* is the quality of the object's surface.

3. How could they draw a sheep to make it look like it has the texture that you described? Give each student a cotton ball. Have students feel the texture of the cotton ball and compare it to the way they think sheep would feel. Explain that sometimes a texture can be created on paper using items that have a feel similar to the one they are describing.

Baa, Baa, Black Sheep *(cont.)*

Art Lesson *(cont.)*

Procedure *(cont.)*

4. Model for the students as you use the "How to Draw a Lamb" page to draw sheep and lambs onto a large piece of white butcher paper. Dip a cotton ball into black paint and dab it onto the body of the sheep. Lay the cotton ball on the newspaper and use another cotton ball to dip into the green paint. Dab the green paint across the bottom, creating a look of soft grass under the sheep's feet. Lay the cotton ball on the newspaper and use another cotton ball to dip into the blue paint. Dip the blue paint above the sheep to represent the sky. Explain that they will use cotton balls to create textures that appear soft.

5. Divide the students into cooperative groups. Explain that they will be creating a mural of black sheep. Give them suggestions such as creating hills with the green paint, making some sheep large and others small, and adding other details with their crayons such as flowers, barns, fences, etc. Explain that since this is a group project, it is important to work together, discussing ideas, and helping each other create an interesting scene.

6. Give each student three cotton balls—one for each color paint. Encourage students to be creative. Allow them to work in their groups as long as possible.

Baa, Baa, Black Sheep *(cont.)*

X,   ex – tra,   have you ex – tra   wool?

Yes   sir!   Yes   sir!   Three   bags   full.

Music Lesson

Skills

- recognizes the sound /x/
- uses rhythm sticks
- knows the hand sign for the letter "x"

Materials

- two rhythm sticks per child (or unsharpened pencils if rhythm sticks are not available)
- butcher paper or chart paper

Before the Lesson

- Copy and enlarge the jingle for the letter "x" onto butcher paper or chart paper.
- Copy and enlarge the nursery rhyme "Baa, Baa, Black Sheep" onto butcher paper or chart paper.

Procedure

1. Read the nursery rhyme "Baa, Baa, Black Sheep" to the class. Read the rhyme a second time, inviting the students to join in as you track the words on the chart.

2. Show students the chart of the jingle for the letter "x." Read the jingle to the class. Explain to the students that this jingle is similar to the nursery rhyme "Baa, Baa, Black Sheep" but that this one will help them to remember the sound that the letter "x" makes as in the word *extra*. Say the jingle together, tracking the words on the chart as they are read.

3. Show the students the hand sign for the letter "x." (See example.) Explain that this is the sign that is used to represent the letter "x" for those who cannot hear or speak. This will also help them to remember "x" as they make this sign during the jingle. Repeat the jingle, using the hand sign for "x" when "x" is read on the chart.

4. Give each student two rhythm sticks or pencils. Explain to students that rhythm sticks are instruments that can be used to tap a beat to music. Invite the students to hold the sticks in the shape of an "x." Have them tap them together, keeping the beat to the jingle for the letter "x." Model for the students how this is done. Allow students to join in, singing the jingle and using their rhythm sticks.

Yankee Doodle

Yankee Doodle

Went to town

Riding on a pony;

Put a feather in his cap

And called it macaroni!

Yankee Doodle *(cont.)*

Art Lesson

Skills

- creates three-dimensional figures
- creates texture
- uses scissors effectively
- uses patterns effectively

Materials

- old socks, one per student
- buttons, two per student
- red, white, and blue yarn
- dowel rod or yard stick, one per student
- batting or cotton stuffing
- permanent marker or black fabric paint
- scissors
- hot glue/hot glue gun
- felt
- ear pattern
- yarn

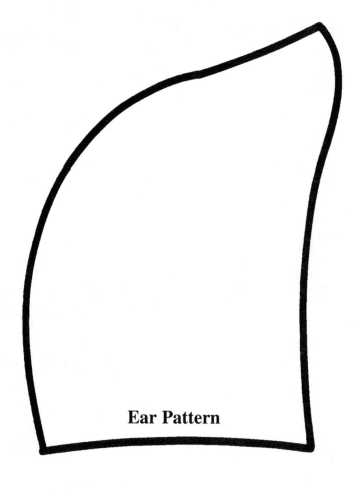

Ear Pattern

Teacher Note: Teachers and other adults should always be at hand to apply hot glue. Students should not use the hot glue guns themselves.

Before the Lesson

1. Copy and enlarge the nursery rhyme "Yankee Doodle" (page 137) onto butcher paper or chart paper.

2. Send home a letter requesting any supplies not readily available for each child. Send the letter home a few days before this lesson.

3. Copy ear patterns on cardstock or trace onto poster board for students to share.

Procedure

1. Read the nursery rhyme "Yankee Doodle" to the class, using the enlarged version. Read the rhyme again, tracking the words as they are read, inviting students to join in if they feel comfortable with the words.

2. Explain that since Yankee Doodle rode a pony, students will need ponies to re-enact the rhyme. Students will make ponies using the old socks that were brought from home. Model each step for the students.

Yankee Doodle *(cont.)*

Art Lesson *(cont.)*

Making Yankee Doodle's Pony

1. Stuff the sock with batting or cotton.

2. Push the dowel rod or yardstick into the opening of the sock about half way.

3. Tie a piece of yarn around the bottom of the sock to hold it in place. Hot glue the underside of the sock to the yardstick. (An adult will need to do this for each student.)

4. Attach buttons for eyes on each side, using a hot glue gun.

5. Draw a mouth with permanent marker or fabric paint.

6. Trace the ear pattern twice on felt. Cut out the ears. Attach the ears on each side of the sock with hot glue.

7. Double a piece of red yarn so that you have two strands approximately 6" (15 cm) long. Tie a knot in the middle. Hot glue the knot to the area between the ears. This is the starting point for the mane that will continue down the back of the neck. Make three red strands, three white strands, and three blue strands in the same manner.

   Encourage students to make all of their knotted strands at once to save time for the teacher who is using the hot glue gun to attach them to each student's horse. Remind them that they will need approximately three of each color.

8. Tie the rope or ribbon around the horse's neck, creating a bridle.

9. Re-enact the rhyme "Yankee Doodle," using your own ponies!

Yankee Doodle *(cont.)*

Y,   Yan - kee   doo-dle dee   dee!

Went   to   town   on his lit - tle po - ny.

Music Lesson

Skills

- recognizes the /y/ sound
- knows the hand sign for the letter "y"
- uses handmade kazoos

Materials

- gum boxes, one per student

Before the Lesson

1. Empty gum boxes before the lesson.
2. Copy and enlarge the jingle for the letter "y" on this page onto butcher paper or chart paper.
3. Copy and enlarge the nursery rhyme "Yankee Doodle" from page 137 onto butcher paper or chart paper.

Procedure

1. Read the nursery rhyme "Yankee Doodle" to the class. Read the rhyme a second time, inviting the students to join in as you track the words on the chart.

2. Show students the chart of the jingle for the letter "y." Read the jingle to the class. Explain to the students that this jingle is similar to the nursery rhyme "Yankee Doodle" but that this one will help them to remember the sound that the letter "y" makes as in *yankee*. Say the jingle together, tracking the words on the chart as they are read.

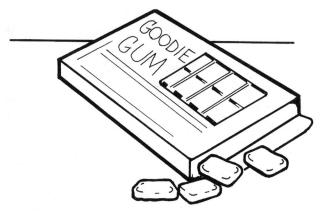

3. Show the students the hand sign for the letter "y." (See example.) Explain that this is the sign that is used to represent the letter "y" for those who cannot hear or speak. This will also help them to remember "y" as they make this sign during the jingle. Say the jingle again, using the hand sign for "y" when "y" is read on the chart.

4. Give each student an empty gum box. Explain that one end of the gum box needs to be open and the other should remain closed. Softly blow into the open end of the box. This will create a buzzing kazoo sound. Divide the class in half. While half of the class sings the jingle, the other half of the class can play their kazoos and vice versa.

This Little Piggie

This little piggie

Went to market,

This little piggie

Stayed at home,

This little piggie

Ate roast beef,

This little piggie ate none,

And this little piggie cried,

Wee, wee, wee,

All the way home.

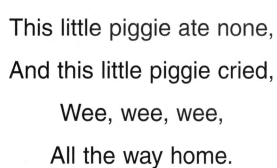

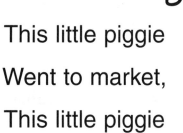

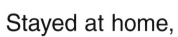

This Little Piggie (cont.)

Art Lesson

Skills

- explores the pliability and dimensionality of clay
- explores the possibilities given by clay
- completes an expressive form appropriate to the student's maturation level
- creates clay

Materials

- flour
- salt
- oil
- water
- wax paper
- large bowl
- red food coloring
- black permanent marker

Before the Lesson

1. Mix several batches of the following recipe so that you have about 1 cup (225 g) of dough for each student.

Dough Recipe

- 2 cups (450 g) flour
- ¼ cup (50 g) salt
- red food coloring
- ½ cup (120 mL) cup water
- ¼ cup (60 mL) oil

Directions

Pour 2 cups of flour in the bowl. Add ¼ cup salt. Stir. Add ¼ cup oil. Add a few drops of red food coloring. Stir. Add ½ cup of water. Stir. The mixture should now be of dough consistency. If it is not, add more flour until it is easy to handle. Knead the dough with your hands, form a ball, and lay it on wax paper.

---

2. Copy and enlarge the nursery rhyme "This Little Piggie" from page 141 onto butcher paper or chart paper and display in the classroom.

Procedure

1. Read the nursery rhyme "This Little Piggie" to the class, using the enlarged version. Read the nursery rhyme a second time, inviting the students to join in reading it with you, tracking the words as they are read.

2. Discuss the nursery rhyme and recall the "footplays" that go along with it, using toes to represent each of the little piggies.

This Little Piggie (cont.)

Art Lesson (cont.)

Procedure (cont.)

3. Explain to the students that they are going to be working with a clay-like art medium. Hand out dough to each student.

4. Explain that they are going to create something that goes with the nursery rhyme out of this pink dough. Can you guess what it is? (*Piggies!*)

5. Demonstrate how to make a piggie to the class.

Making a Piggie

1. Pull off a small amount of dough and roll it into a ball to create the head.
2. Pull off a smaller piece of dough and roll it into a ball for the snout. Press it on the head.
3. Pull off two more small pieces and press them on the head as ears.
4. Pull off a large piece of dough and roll into an oval for the body. Press the head onto the body.
5. Use a pencil to press two holes in the snout and two holes for eyes.
6. Pull off four more medium pieces for the legs. Roll them one at a time on the table until they are the right size and press them under the body.
7. Finally, pull off a small piece and roll it out for the tail. Make it look curly if you can!

This Little Piggie *(cont.)*

Z, ze – ro roast beef had he,

for the lit – tle pig who went wee, wee, wee!

Music Lesson

Skills

- recognizes the /z/ sound
- knows the hand sign for the letter "z"
- demonstrates vowel sound recognition

Before the Lesson

1. Copy and enlarge the jingle for the letter "z" on this page onto butcher paper or chart paper.
2. Copy and enlarge the nursery rhyme "This Little Piggie" from page 141 onto butcher paper or chart paper.
3. Write each vowel—A, E, I, O, U—onto a large piece of construction paper.

Procedure

1. Read the nursery rhyme "This Little Piggie" to the class. Read the rhyme a second time, inviting the students to join in as you track the words on the chart.
2. Show students the chart of the jingle for the letter "z." Read the jingle to the class. Explain to the students that this jingle is similar to the nursery rhyme "This Little Piggie" but that this will help them to remember the sound that the letter "z" makes as in *zero*. Say the jingle together, tracking the words on the chart as they are read.
3. Show the students the hand sign for the letter "z." (See example.) Explain that this is the sign that is used to represent the letter "z" for those who cannot hear or speak. This will also help them to remember "z" as they make this sign during the jingle. Repeat the jingle, using the hand sign for "z" when "z" is read on the chart.

4. Introduce the students to the five vowels, A, E, I, O, and U. Hold up each letter card and say the long vowel sound of each. Have students repeat each sound back. Explain to the students that the little pig went "wee wee wee " all the way home. Ask them which vowel sound is heard at the end of wee.
5. Share with the students that the jingle's words will be changed slightly with the different vowels. Substitute the long E sound in the word *wee* for the long A sound in the word *way* (wā). Have students sing the jingle, using that substitution. Hold up a different letter card. Substitute the long vowel sound on the card for *wee* again. Continue this procedure until all vowel sounds have been practiced.